AUTOCAD® 2000 FOR DUMMIES®

Quick Reference

by Ellen Finkelstein

IDG Books Worldwide, Inc.
An International Data Group Company

Foster City, CA ✦ Chicago, IL ✦ Indianapolis, IN ✦ New York, NY

AutoCAD® 2000 For Dummies® Quick Reference

Published by
IDG Books Worldwide, Inc.
An International Data Group Company
919 E. Hillsdale Blvd.
Suite 400
Foster City, CA 94404
www.idgbooks.com (IDG Books Worldwide Web site)
www.dummies.com (Dummies Press Web site)

Library of Congress Catalog Card No.: 99-63214

ISBN: 0-7645-0559-9

Printed in the United States of America

10 9 8 7 6 5 4 3 2 1

1P/SQ/QX/ZZ/IN

Distributed in the United States by IDG Books Worldwide, Inc.

Distributed by CDG Books Canada Inc. for Canada; by Transworld Publishers Limited in the United Kingdom; by IDG Norge Books for Norway; by IDG Sweden Books for Sweden; by Woodslane Pty. Ltd. for Australia; by Woodslane (NZ) Ltd. for New Zealand; by TransQuest Publishers Pte Ltd. for Singapore, Malaysia, Thailand, Indonesia, and Hong Kong; by ICG Muse, Inc. for Japan; by Norma Comunicaciones S.A. for Colombia; by Intersoft for South Africa; by Eyrolles for France; by International Thomson Publishing for Germany, Austria and Switzerland; by Distribuidora Cuspide for Argentina; by Livraria Cultura for Brazil; by Ediciones ZETA S.C.R. Ltda. for Peru; by WS Computer Publishing Corporation, Inc., for the Philippines; by Contemporanea de Ediciones for Venezuela; by Express Computer Distributors for the Caribbean and West Indies; by Micronesia Media Distributor, Inc. for Micronesia; by Grupo Editorial Norma S.A. for Guatemala; by Chips Computadoras S.A. de C.V. for Mexico; by Editorial Norma de Panama S.A. for Panama; by American Bookshops for Finland. Authorized Sales Agent: Anthony Rudkin Associates for the Middle East and North Africa.

For general information on IDG Books Worldwide's books in the U.S., please call our Consumer Customer Service department at 800-762-2974. For reseller information, including discounts and premium sales, please call our Reseller Customer Service department at 800-434-3422.

For information on where to purchase IDG Books Worldwide's books outside the U.S., please contact our International Sales department at 317-596-5530 or fax 317-596-5692.

For consumer information on foreign language translations, please contact our Customer Service department at 1-800-434-3422, fax 317-596-5692, or e-mail rights@idgbooks.com.

For information on licensing foreign or domestic rights, please phone +1-650-655-3109.

For sales inquiries and special prices for bulk quantities, please contact our Sales department at 650-655-3200 or write to the address above.

For information on using IDG Books Worldwide's books in the classroom or for ordering examination copies, please contact our Educational Sales department at 800-434-2086 or fax 317-596-5499.

For press review copies, author interviews, or other publicity information, please contact our Public Relations department at 650-655-3000 or fax 650-655-3299.

For authorization to photocopy items for corporate, personal, or educational use, please contact Copyright Clearance Center, 222 Rosewood Drive, Danvers, MA 01923, or fax 978-750-4470.

About the Author

Ellen Finkelstein learned AutoCAD in Israel, where she was always the one responsible for poring over the AutoCAD manual because it was in English. After drafting and then teaching AutoCAD there, she returned to the United States and started consulting and teaching AutoCAD as well as other computer programs, including Microsoft Word, Excel, and PowerPoint. Besides this book, she has written two other books on AutoCAD. One of them, *AutoCAD 2000 Bible,* weighing in at about 1,200 pages (who's counting?), is also published by IDG Books Worldwide, Inc. She was also a contributing author for *AutoCAD 13 SECRETS* and has written books on Microsoft Word and PowerPoint. She is an Autodesk registered author and an Autodesk Certified Professional. She writes at home so she can take the bread out of the oven on time.

ABOUT IDG BOOKS WORLDWIDE

Welcome to the world of IDG Books Worldwide.

IDG Books Worldwide, Inc., is a subsidiary of International Data Group, the world's largest publisher of computer-related information and the leading global provider of information services on information technology. IDG was founded more than 30 years ago by Patrick J. McGovern and now employs more than 9,000 people worldwide. IDG publishes more than 290 computer publications in over 75 countries. More than 90 million people read one or more IDG publications each month.

Launched in 1990, IDG Books Worldwide is today the #1 publisher of best-selling computer books in the United States. We are proud to have received eight awards from the Computer Press Association in recognition of editorial excellence and three from Computer Currents' First Annual Readers' Choice Awards. Our best-selling ...For Dummies® series has more than 50 million copies in print with translations in 31 languages. IDG Books Worldwide, through a joint venture with IDG's Hi-Tech Beijing, became the first U.S. publisher to publish a computer book in the People's Republic of China. In record time, IDG Books Worldwide has become the first choice for millions of readers around the world who want to learn how to better manage their businesses.

Our mission is simple: Every one of our books is designed to bring extra value and skill-building instructions to the reader. Our books are written by experts who understand and care about our readers. The knowledge base of our editorial staff comes from years of experience in publishing, education, and journalism — experience we use to produce books to carry us into the new millennium. In short, we care about books, so we attract the best people. We devote special attention to details such as audience, interior design, use of icons, and illustrations. And because we use an efficient process of authoring, editing, and desktop publishing our books electronically, we can spend more time ensuring superior content and less time on the technicalities of making books.

You can count on our commitment to deliver high-quality books at competitive prices on topics you want to read about. At IDG Books Worldwide, we continue in the IDG tradition of delivering quality for more than 30 years. You'll find no better book on a subject than one from IDG Books Worldwide.

John Kilcullen
Chairman and CEO
IDG Books Worldwide, Inc.

Steven Berkowitz
President and Publisher
IDG Books Worldwide, Inc.

Eighth Annual Computer Press Awards ≥1992

WINNER
Ninth Annual Computer Press Awards ≥1993

WINNER
Tenth Annual Computer Press Awards ≥1994

WINNER
Eleventh Annual Computer Press Awards ≥1995

Dedication

To MMY, who taught me how to find my inner intelligence so I could understand AutoCAD and write clearly about it — and my inner creativity so I could be funny.

Author's Acknowledgments

First, I would like to thank my husband, Evan, for his incredible support while I wrote this book (and two others at the same time). He did the laundry, went shopping, and put the kids to bed while I sat in front of the computer. Thanks to my kids, Yeshayah and Eliyah, who understood — most of the time. My parents also have my appreciation for teaching me that I could do anything (even write a book about AutoCAD, of all things).

Thanks to everyone at IDG Books Worldwide who helped create this book. Steve Hayes got the book rolling and was supportive when I demanded a $1 million advance. Susan Pink coordinated the entire process from her hideaway in Maine. She was cool when I pleaded that I couldn't make my deadlines and funny when we were under the greatest pressure. Thanks, Susan! I also want to thank all the others at IDG who helped put the book together.

Thanks to Dennis Shinn, the technical editor, who was thorough and knowledgeable. His comments helped make the book more complete and precise.

Publisher's Acknowledgments

We're proud of this book; please send us your comments through our IDG Books Worldwide Online Registration Form located at http:// my2cents.dummies.com. Some of the people who helped bring this book to market include the following:

Acquisitions, Editorial, and Media Development

Project Editor: Susan Pink
(*Previous Edition:* Kelly Oliver)

Acquisitions Editor:
Steven H. Hayes

Technical Editor: Dennis Shinn

Editorial Manager: Mary C. Corder

Editorial Assistant: Beth Parlon

Production

Project Coordinator: E. Shawn Aylsworth

Layout and Graphics: Angela F. Hunckler, Dave McKelvey, Barry Offringa, Brent Savage, Jacque Schneider

Proofreaders: Christine Sabooni, Marianne Santy

Indexer: Liz Cunningham

Special Help: Suzanne Thomas

General and Administrative

IDG Books Worldwide, Inc.: John Kilcullen, CEO; Steven Berkowitz, President and Publisher

IDG Books Technology Publishing: Brenda McLaughlin, Senior Vice President and Group Publisher

Dummies Technology Press and Dummies Editorial: Diane Graves Steele, Vice President and Associate Publisher; Mary Bednarek, Director of Acquisitions and Product Development; Kristin A. Cocks, Editorial Director

Dummies Trade Press: Kathleen A. Welton, Vice President and Publisher; Kevin Thornton, Acquisitions Manager

IDG Books Production for Dummies Press: Michael R. Britton, Vice President of Production; Debbie Stailey, Associate Director of Production; Cindy L. Phipps, Manager of Project Coordination, Production Proofreading, and Indexing; Shelley Lea, Supervisor of Graphics and Design; Debbie J. Gates, Production Systems Specialist; Robert Springer, Supervisor of Proofreading; Laura Carpenter, Production Control Manager; Tony Augsburger, Supervisor of Reprints and Bluelines

Dummies Packaging and Book Design: Patty Page, Manager, Promotions Marketing

◆

The publisher would like to give special thanks to Patrick J. McGovern, without whom this book would not have been possible.

◆

able of Contents

How to Use This Book

I'm Nobody

I'm nobody! Who are you?

Are you nobody, too?

Then there's a pair of us — don't tell!

They'd advertise, you know.

—Emily Dickinson

This book is for us nobodies — normal people who want or need to use AutoCAD without having to be an engineer or a programmer. (Even those engineers and programmers among you must have a normal side!) Sure, AutoCAD is complex, but it doesn't have to be scary. This book organizes a vast amount of information about AutoCAD for you, so that you can read only the parts that you need to read, stay blissfully unaware of the rest, and still do your job.

Who Needs This Book

This book is useful for beginning and intermediate AutoCAD users. I cover the vast majority of commands in AutoCAD 2000, including how to use each command and what those obscure AutoCAD terms mean.

AutoCAD 2000 For Dummies Quick Reference is, as the name implies, a reference book. For more information, a great place to start is with *AutoCAD 2000 For Dummies* by Bud Smith (IDG Books Worldwide, Inc.); it's informative, easy to read, and (most importantly) funny! When you're ready for a full-length, comprehensive reference, I'm not too shy to recommend my own tome, *AutoCAD 2000 Bible*, also published by IDG Books Worldwide, Inc.

After you start using AutoCAD, this book is the one to keep by your computer all the time. No one can know everything about AutoCAD, so you'll always need to look things up. That's okay! (Now that you know the secret — that even advanced users continue to look up things about AutoCAD — you won't feel so self-conscious when you do it.)

How I Stuffed All of AutoCAD into This Tiny Book

I actually included almost all the AutoCAD commands, including all regular 2D, 3D, and rendering commands. What did I leave out? Well, because this book is a Quick Reference, I felt that I couldn't do justice to some subjects in a short format. Those subjects are the commands related to LISP (AutoCAD's programming language), customizing AutoCAD (such as writing script files or customizing menus), and the DBCONNECT command for connecting to external databases.

Also, I covered each command only briefly (remember, this book is a reference, not a long-winded technical explanation). I tell you *how* to use the command by walking you through the options, suboptions, and sometimes sub-suboptions.

Those Little Icons

AutoCAD 2000 For Dummies Quick Reference is loaded with icons that give you an instant impression of a topic, so you can decide whether it's the one that you want.

This book covers some advanced commands and technical stuff. This icon informs you before you take the plunge.

On the other hand, some commands are easy as pie. This icon tells you that you can take a sigh of relief.

This icon indicates features that are new or significantly changed in AutoCAD 2000.

This icon warns you of problem areas that can mess up your work.

This icon points out clever AutoCAD tricks to help you along the way.

This icon directs you to more details in *AutoCAD 2000 For Dummies* by Bud Smith (IDG Books Worldwide, Inc.) or elsewhere in this book.

How This Book Is Organized

Because this is a reference book, the material is organized for easy look-up. And although your sixth-grade teacher probably told you not to do this, I give you permission to fold down the corner of any pages you want.

Part I: The Basics

This part gives you the basics that you can't find under any command. The part includes brief sections on getting started, using commands, setting up a drawing, specifying points, viewing your drawing, selecting objects, organizing your drawing with layers, using Help, and getting in and out of drawings safely and efficiently. As necessary, I refer you to the appropriate command in Part II.

Part II: The Commands

This part is an alphabetical listing of all (well, almost all) the commands. I don't expect you to read this part through from beginning to end — although it's okay if you want to. Part II is the main reference section; just look up the command that you need.

Part III: The System Variables

Part III lists the system variables not controlled using any command and a few especially useful system variables. As AutoCAD slowly improves its interface, more of the system variables are handled in dialog boxes, but you still may want to type some of them in the command line. I organized these variables by function so that you can find them easily.

Part IV: The Toolbars

If you know that you want to do some task but don't know the command name, you can look in this part. The toolbars are organized by type of task (Draw, Modify, and so on).

Part V: Techie Talk

You've heard of Newspeak (from George Orwell's *1984*)? Well, AutoCAD has AutoSpeak. I include words that have unique meanings in the AutoCAD world so you can figure it all out.

Part I

The Basics

If you're a new AutoCAD user, be sure to read this part;
you'll find out how to get started and review the basics
you need to understand the unique world of AutoCAD.
If you're already familiar with AutoCAD, you might want
to skim through; you'll know most of this stuff, but
you're sure to find something new. At the very least,
look for the AutoCAD 2000 icons to get yourself up to
speed on the latest and the greatest.

Throughout this part, I refer as necessary to
commands listed in Part II.

In this part . . .

✔ **Looking at the AutoCAD screen**

✔ **Giving AutoCAD orders**

✔ **Setting up a drawing**

✔ **Specifying coordinates**

✔ **Selecting objects for editing**

✔ **Getting help**

✔ **Leaving a drawing and AutoCAD**

✔ **Finding out what's new**

Getting Started

It's good to start at the beginning, and you start by launching AutoCAD. After installing AutoCAD, you can start by choosing Start➪Programs➪AutoCAD 2000. Sharp operators, however, know that opening AutoCAD from a shortcut on the desktop is easier. To create a shortcut, follow these steps:

1. Double-click My Computer from the desktop.

2. Find acad.exe (it's probably in the ACAD2000 folder) and right-click it.

3. Choose Make Shortcut. You see a new icon that reads *shortcut to acad.exe*.

4. Drag the icon to your desktop.

5. Click the icon's name and type any new name you want. Press Enter.

You can now double-click the icon to open AutoCAD. Much better!

 See Appendix A of *AutoCAD 2000 For Dummies* by Bud Smith (published by IDG Books Worldwide, Inc.) for some help on installing AutoCAD.

Opening a new or an existing drawing

 When you start AutoCAD, you see the Startup dialog box with four choices:

✦ Open a Drawing. Choose an existing drawing to work on.

✦ Start from Scratch. Start a new drawing with only the basic default settings.

✦ Use a Template. Choose a template as a basis for a new drawing. Templates are covered later in this chapter, too.

✦ Use a Wizard. Walk through the process of setting up a drawing, covered later in this part.

Whichever you choose, you find yourself magically transported into a new or existing drawing. You can click your heels to get home or just start drawing.

After you've worked on a drawing, you can open a new drawing by clicking New on the Standard toolbar. You can open an existing drawing by clicking Open on the Standard toolbar.

Finally, AutoCAD lets you open more than one drawing at a time, like every other Windows application.

See also the OPEN and the NEW commands in Part II.

The AutoCAD screen

Here's the way your screen looks when you open AutoCAD.

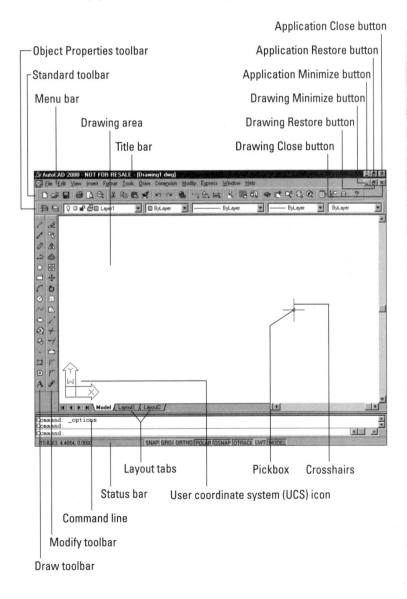

Application Close button

Object Properties toolbar — Application Restore button

Standard toolbar — Application Minimize button

Menu bar — Drawing Minimize button

Drawing area — Drawing Restore button

Title bar — Drawing Close button

Layout tabs — Pickbox — Crosshairs

Status bar — User coordinate system (UCS) icon

Command line

Modify toolbar

Draw toolbar

At the very top is the title bar, which tells you that you're in AutoCAD (in case you were confused) and gives you the name of your drawing. If you've opened a new drawing and haven't named it yet, the title bar lists the drawing as Drawing1.dwg.

The next row is the menu bar. Use the menus in this bar to choose commands.

Below the menu bar is the Standard toolbar. This toolbar contains many of the most commonly used commands. The Object Properties toolbar comes next. Use it to control layers, linetypes, lineweights, and colors. On the left of the screen, you see the Draw and Modify toolbars.

You, the magician, can make many more toolbars appear by right-clicking any toolbar and choosing the toolbar you want from the list that appears. Some toolbars have secondary menus called *flyouts*; you find one by clicking any icon that has a little black arrow in the corner and holding down the mouse button until the flyout buttons fly out.

The big space in the middle is where you draw. Here you see a small crosshair with a pickbox at its center. The crosshair represents the cursor while you are drawing.

Below the drawing area is the command line, where you can type commands, options, and values such as the length of a radius.

The status bar is at the bottom. Click the buttons on the status bar to control drawing aids and other features of AutoCAD. These are discussed later in this part.

Save me, save me!

It may seem funny that I'm talking about saving before I talk about drawing anything, but it's never too early to find out how to save. Use the QSAVE command (click Save on the Standard toolbar) frequently to save your drawing. The first time you save a new, unnamed drawing, AutoCAD opens a dialog box so that you can name your drawing.

Furthermore, I recommend setting AutoCAD to save your drawing automatically at regular intervals. You know that the only time you forget to save is right before your computer crashes. Now that you can open multiple drawings at once, you can lose your work from more drawings than ever before! Choose Tools⇨Options⇨and click the Open and Save tab of the Options dialog box. Check the Automatic Save check box and type the time interval you want. The default is a ridiculous 120 minutes. Whoever thought you wouldn't mind redoing two hours of work if AutoCAD crashes is a little nuts. Change the setting to 15 or 30 minutes — max.

Ordering AutoCAD Around

I don't know what the AutoCAD menus really do at night when we're not looking, but they do seem to multiply. AutoCAD has the screen menu, the menu bar, the tablet menu, the button menu, the cursor menu, and the toolbars. And, of course, there's the ever-present command line, which you can use if you hate menus.

Pointing devices: mouse or digitizer

Most people use a mouse with AutoCAD. Some people use a digitizing tablet, which usually works with a *puck*. The left button on your mouse is the *pick* button, which means that you pick things with it — a menu item, a toolbar button, or an object you've drawn. The right button opens shortcut menus, ends the process of object selection, and sometimes ends commands. If your mouse has more than two buttons, try them out to see what they do. You may like what you find.

The command line

You can enter all commands by simply typing them on the command line at the bottom of the screen. So even though Part II tells you how to access each command using a menu or a toolbar, you can always type the command name in the command line. If your goal is to get away from the command line completely, better choose another goal. Often, a command that starts with a menu or a toolbar button reverts to the command line for you to input coordinates, values, or command options.

After you have started a command, you can choose a command option by right-clicking and choosing the option you want from the shortcut menu.

Options are also listed on the command line, separated by slashes (/). If you want, you can choose options by typing on the command line. One or more letters of the option are capitalized. You need type only the capitalized letter or letters of the option to choose the option. The command's default, if any, appears in angled brackets (< >). Press Enter to choose the default.

Every time you need to type something on the command line — such as the name of a command, an option, coordinates, or values — you must press Enter afterward. You can also press the spacebar if that's easier for you.

Transparent commands are commands that you use while you're in the middle of another command. You can use transparently almost every command that doesn't draw or modify an object. When typing a transparent command on the command line, precede it with an apostrophe, as in 'zoom. The buttons on the status bar also function like transparent commands.

After you use a command, you can repeat it by pressing Enter. If you start a command and change your mind, press the Esc key. You can use the F2 key to open the text screen and see more of the command-line history. Pressing F2 again gets you back to the drawing screen.

If you type a complex coordinate and see that you've made a mistake, you don't have to type the whole darn thing over. Just use the arrow keys to move back to the mistake. Use either the Backspace key to erase your entry to the left of the cursor or the Del key to erase your entry to the right of the cursor. To repeat the previous command-line entry, press the Up arrow key and then press Enter.

All the pretty little menus and toolbars

Using the mouse to start commands in AutoCAD is convenient. You're looking at the screen as you draw, and you don't need to look down at the keyboard or anywhere else. The commands are right there, where you're drawing.

The menus are easy to use. An ellipsis (...) after an item means that the item opens a dialog box. An arrow means that suboptions pop out from the item. The nice items with nothing after them execute a command for you without any further delay.

Although most people use the mouse to access a menu, you can use the keyboard. Hold down the Alt key and press whichever letter is underlined in the menu. Then press the letter that is underlined on the item you want.

AutoCAD also has shortcut menus, which you get to by right-clicking. Just to confuse you, the shortcut menu that appears depends on where your cursor is and whether or not you have a command active or an object selected. Shortcut menus appear at the cursor, so they are sometimes called cursor menus. You can customize these menus (and all other menus, as well) — if you're into that.

A word about toolbars: You can't use AutoCAD efficiently without knowing how to use the toolbars. Most toolbars are hidden until you command them to show themselves. (Right-click any toolbar and choose the toolbar you want.) *See also* Part IV for the complete set of toolbars.

Dialog boxes

Some commands open dialog boxes. Usually, these dialog boxes are fairly simple to understand — and easier to understand than the same operation on the command line. Choose the options you want and click OK. (Sometimes you click Save or Open.) Some dialog boxes offer *image tiles* that enable you to see the results of your choices. When I have the choice of using a dialog box or the command line, I go with the dialog box. To get help on any item in a dialog box, click the question mark, and then click the item.

It's a Setup!

This section explains how to set up a drawing. AutoCAD is famous for the extent of its customizability — the setup described here is just one example. Before you draw, you need to make some preparations for efficient drawing, and that's what this section is all about.

The template

When you open a new drawing using the Use a Template option, AutoCAD asks you to choose a template. The template automatically selected is `acad -named plot styles.dwt`. (Yes, the name is a little awkward.) You can change the settings of this template to whatever you want. Most offices have standards for the majority of these settings.

Using a template is a great time-saver, because you don't have to create these settings every time you start a new drawing. For example, you can create layers (with the LAYER command) and create text and dimension styles (with the STYLE and DIMSTYLE commands). To customize the default template or create a new template, follow these steps:

1. Open a new drawing using the Start from Scratch option if you don't want any extraneous settings. Or open an existing drawing that has most or all the settings you want. (If you use an existing drawing, erase any unwanted objects.) To customize the default template, open it by choosing Drawing Template File in the File of Type drop-down list of the Open dialog box. You can use the Wizard option if you want.

2. Create the settings you want, by using either the Wizard or the individual commands.

3. Choose File⇨Save if you're in a new drawing. Choose File⇨ Save As if you're working from an existing, named drawing.

4. In the Save Drawing As dialog box, click the Save as Type drop-down arrow. Choose Drawing Template File (*.dwt).

5. The dialog box lists the current templates in the \Template folder. If you want to customize `acad -named plot styles.dwt` or another existing template, choose it. Otherwise, give your template a new name in the File Name text box.

6. Click Save.

To use the template, choose Use a Template in the Startup dialog box, choose your template, and click OK.

You can create several templates. You might want to insert a title block and border for each size of drawing you use. That way, when you start a new drawing, everything is set up for you.

Wiz with the Wizard

When you start AutoCAD, if you don't have a template that you want to use, you can choose Use a Wizard to go through the process of setting up a drawing. You can choose a quick setup to select only your unit of measurement type and drawing limits. Choose the advanced setup to include drawing layout and paper space options. You can also use individual commands to create the same effect, as explained in the next few sections. Save all these settings in your template.

Units

If you don't use a template or the Wizard when you set up a drawing, one of the first things you might want to use is the UNITS command. With this command, you decide such basics as whether your measurements will be in decimals or in feet and inches, and how precisely the measurements will be displayed. You can also set your units of measurement for angles.

Layer upon layer

Layers are *very* important. They organize the objects in your drawings by color and linetype (continuous, dotted, dashed, and so on), and lineweight (width). Layers make sure that all dimensions have the same color or all center lines use the same color and linetype so your drawing is easier to understand.

If you use AutoCAD at work, your office probably has standards for layers so that all drawings use the same layers for the same types of objects. Write down these standards and make them available to everyone. Create layers using the LAYER command (choose Layer from the Object Properties toolbar).

After you define your layers, you can make a layer current by choosing it from the Layer Control drop-down list on the Object Properties toolbar. Anything you draw is on the current layer. Another way to change the current layer is to pick an object that's on the layer you want to make current. Then, on the Object Properties toolbar, click Make Object's Layer Current.

The Object Properties toolbar works somewhat like the Formatting toolbar on your word processor. When no object is selected, the Layer, Color, Linetype, Lineweight, and Plot Style drop-down lists display the current layer, color, linetype, lineweight, and plot style. But when an object is selected, the Object Properties toolbar displays the properties of the selected object.

Stylish writing

When the time comes to annotate your drawing, you need to get into text styles. Your office may have some standards regarding text styles — you don't want some drawings using a plain font and others using a font with lots of curlicues.

A text style includes the font, the height (optionally), the character width, and other text attributes. You create text styles with the STYLE command. When you create a style, it becomes the current style. The DTEXT/TEXT and MTEXT commands have a Style option so that you can specify the style before you type your text.

Cool dimensions

Dimension styles are complex. You're lucky if someone else has gone through all those dialog box tabs and created a dimension style for you. If not, look up the DIMSTYLE command in Part II. Then use any of the dimension commands (all of them start with *DIM*) to start creating dimensions.

Creating a user coordinate system (UCS)

If you're into 3D, you can set up your coordinates anywhere and in any direction and orientation you want. (You can do so for a 2D drawing, but it's not as necessary.) The default UCS is called the world coordinate system (WCS), where the X axis is horizontal, the Y axis is vertical, and the Z axis extends perpendicularly out from the screen (right into your forehead). If you're drawing an angled roof for a house, however, you can set the origin to the bottom-left corner of the roof and angle the X,Y-coordinates so that they match the edges and angle of the roof. That procedure makes drawing a skylight in the roof a lot easier. *See also* the UCS command in Part II.

After you create a user coordinate system (UCS), you can save it for later use. Once you have your UCS, all coordinates are based on the origin and axes you defined in your UCS.

Getting Picky: Specifying Points

You're going to spend a lot of time specifying the coordinates of the objects you draw. Coordinates are based on a Cartesian coordinate system, with X and Y (and Z, for 3D) axes. Positive numbers go to the right and up from the origin (0,0); negative numbers (because of their sins) go in the other direction. The convention for specifying coordinates is to type the X-coordinate first, then a comma, and then the Y-coordinate. The figure shows a few coordinates.

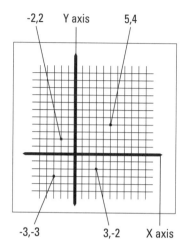

You can specify coordinates in several ways. The simplest way is to pick a point on-screen with your mouse. But that method may not be the most accurate. You might need to type coordinates to get the necessary precision.

Displaying coordinates

Before you start typing coordinates, knowing where you are helps. AutoCAD helpfully displays coordinates in the status bar. AutoCAD has three types of coordinate display: *static,* which shows only points that you specify; *dynamic,* which moves as the cursor moves; and *distance<angle,* which also moves as the cursor moves. The distance<angle display appears only while you're using a command in which you need to specify more than one point, such as when you are drawing a line or moving an object. You toggle among these displays by pressing the F6 key or Ctrl+D. Get into the habit of looking at those coordinates so that you don't get lost!

Oodles of coordinates

You can specify coordinates in five ways; as you get used to them, you know which is the right one to use in your particular situation. Two types of coordinates are used only for 3D.

Absolute Cartesian coordinates are called *absolute* because they're based on the X,Y-coordinate system. The point is (no pun intended — well, maybe I did intend a little . . .) that absolute coordinates are relative to the 0,0 point of your X and Y axes — as in 3,4. If drawing in 3D, add the Z-axis-coordinate.

Often you don't know the absolute coordinate, but you know the change in X and Y from your last point, such as the start point of the line you're drawing. Here's where *relative Cartesian coordinates* can help. Relative coordinates are relative to the last point you drew. You tell AutoCAD that you're using a relative coordinate by typing the @ symbol in front of the coordinates, as in @3,4. If you're drawing in 3D, add the Z-axis-coordinate.

Very often, all you know is how long your line is supposed to be and in what direction it should go. *Polar coordinates* to the rescue! Polar coordinates can be both relative and absolute. These coordinates define a point in terms of a distance (the length of your line, for example) and an angle.

The format for absolute polar coordinates is *length<angle,* as in 6<30, which would draw a line six units long at an angle of 30 degrees. Relative polar coordinates are measured relative to the last point you drew and require the @ symbol.

You start counting zero degrees along the positive X axis, and angles are measured counterclockwise from there. (If you're into weird angle measurements, you can change how they're measured by using the UNITS command.) You can type negative angles to measure clockwise, so that @neg90 degrees is the same as 270 degrees.

Cylindrical coordinates are the 3D version of polar coordinates. (If 3D drafting makes you run in the opposite direction, just skip this section.) They can also be absolute or relative. Cylindrical coordinates can be confusing because the lengths indicate not the length of the line (or whatever you're drawing), as polar coordinates do, but the number of units in two directions.

The format for absolute cylindrical coordinates is *distance<angle, distance,* as in 6<30,4. The first distance is the number of units in the XY plane. The angle is the number of degrees from the X axis in the XY plane. With these two points, you have defined a point on the XY plane. Now comes the last distance, the number of units along the Z axis, which defines the point in three dimensions. (Don't forget to use the @ symbol if you're specifying the coordinate relative to the last point you entered.)

Spherical coordinates are like cylindrical ones, except that instead of a second distance, you use a second angle. Got it?

The format for absolute spherical coordinates is *distance<angle <angle,* as in 6<30<45. The distance is the number of units from the origin or your last point. The first angle is the angle from the X axis in the XY plane. The second angle is the angle up from the XY plane (in the Z direction). Spherical coordinates indicate the actual distance, so a line drawn from 0,0 to 6<30<45, for example, is 6 units long. Use the @ symbol for relative spherical coordinates.

Object snaps

If the coordinate you want is on an object, you often can use *object snaps,* which are geometric points on objects. For example, you can move the endpoint of one line to the midpoint of another using object snaps. Anytime AutoCAD asks you for a point, you can use an object snap. You can use an object snap for just one command, or you can set running object snaps that continue until you turn them off. See the OSNAP command (that's object snaps in Autospeak) for details on setting running snaps.

You can choose an object snap in several ways. Probably the best way is to use the object snap shortcut menu (press Shift and right-click). Also, the Standard toolbar has an Object Snap flyout that contains icons for each object snap type. If you're typing coordinates anyway, you can type the object snap abbreviation. (Try typing the first three letters; that method usually works.)

The object snaps are *endpoint, midpoint, intersection, apparent inter-section, extension, center, quadrant, node, insertion, perpendicular, tangent, nearest, parallel, quick,* and *none.* Obviously, some object snaps are appropriate only for certain objects. Only circles, arcs, and ellipses have a center, for example. *Insertion* means the inser-tion point of text and blocks.

The AutoSnap feature lets you know when you're near an object snap that you've turned on (by setting it as a running object snap or choosing it just for the current command). You see a SnapTip that labels the object snap and a marker that shows the location of the object snap. Each object snap has its own marker shape. There's also a magnetic pull that draws the cursor to the object snap that it loves. If you want a specific object snap and several are in the neighborhood, press Tab repeatedly to cycle through the object snaps. You can use the OSNAP button on the status bar to turn running object snaps on and off instantly.

From here, there, everywhere

But what if the point you want to specify isn't on an object, but near it? *From* isn't really an object snap, although you can find it in all the same places that object snaps lurk. The From feature is a way to specify a point that's a certain distance (called an offset) from a point you can more easily specify. Suppose you have two existing lines and want to start a new line at the point in the middle of the figure.

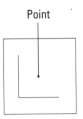

Point

Start the LINE command, and at the Specify first point: prompt, choose From in the object snap shortcut. You can also find From on the Object Snap flyout of the Standard toolbar, or you can simply type it on the command line. AutoCAD asks you for a base point. In this case, you could use the intersection object snap to choose the intersection of the existing lines. Then AutoCAD asks you for the offset. If the point is 1 unit to the right (the X distance) and 1 unit up from the base point (the Y distance), type @1,1. (You can use any type of relative coordinates.) AutoCAD starts the line right where you want it and you can now finish your line.

Tracking down the elusive point

Object snap tracking enables you to locate a new point based on the coordinates of object snaps on existing objects. This feature is a way to track down coordinates and use them to create a new coordinate. It's meant for only 2D drafting.

In AutoCAD 2000, you pass your cursor over points to *acquire* them. You then see a small plus sign at the points. As you draw or edit, AutoCAD displays temporary alignment paths extending from the cursor to the acquired points. You can use these alignment paths to find the intersection of two acquired points, for example.

In the figure, suppose you want to draw a line from the point.

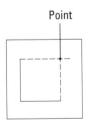

Point

Do you see how the point has the same X-coordinate as the horizontal line and the same Y-coordinate as the vertical line? Another way to look at it is to consider two imaginary lines perpendicular to each of the existing lines (shown by the dashed lines). These lines would intersect right at the point you want.

To use object snap tracking, click the Otrack button on the status bar. Then start a command (in this case, the LINE command) and, when AutoCAD asks you for a point, pass your cursor over the right endpoint of the horizontal line and the top endpoint of the vertical line. You have now acquired these two endpoints. Now move the cursor in the direction of the desired point (that's important) until you see the temporary alignment paths and the SnapTip listing both endpoints. Then click. Mission accomplished!

In the preceding example, you tracked based on only 90-degree angles. You can track at other angles, too, using polar tracking. Right-click the Polar button on the status bar and choose Settings. In the Drafting Settings dialog box, choose an angle from the Increment Angle drop-down list. For example, if you choose 45.0 from the list, you can track at 45°, 90°, 135°, 180°, 225°, and so on. Then click Track Using All Polar Angle Settings and click OK. Make sure the Polar button is "pushed" in. For more information, see the DSETTINGS command in Part II.

Filters

Point filters enable you to extract all or part of a coordinate from an object. This capability helps when the coordinate that you need isn't obvious. (Yes, it's similar to tracking. It's slower but sometimes more precise. And it's a necessity for 3D drawing.) The format is a period (.) and one or two axis letters. Whichever filter you use, AutoCAD prompts you for the *other* axis value(s).

Using the same figure as in the "Tracking down the elusive point" section, start the LINE command. At the Specify first point: prompt, type **.x** and then press Enter. AutoCAD responds with the of prompt, meaning, "What do you want to find the X-coordinate of?" In this example, you use an endpoint object snap to pick the right endpoint of the existing horizontal line. Now AutoCAD responds with the (need YZ): prompt. Pick the endpoint of the existing vertical line. (Ignore the request for a Z-coordinate if you're drawing in 2D.) AutoCAD locates your point and you can continue to draw your line.

SNAP to it!

Turning on snap restricts the cursor to points on an invisible grid. When you turn on snap, you set the size of the grid. If you turn on snap at .5, for example, the cursor jumps to points every half-unit apart; anything in between is off-limits. To turn the snap on and off, click SNAP on the status bar. To set the snap size, right click SNAP on the status bar and choose Settings.

If your drawing has lots of complex coordinates, such as (3.165,4.2798), snap won't help you. But if you use simpler coordinates, such as (3.25,6.5), snap is for you. Turning on snap enables you to draw without typing coordinates. You just watch those coordinates in the status bar and, when you have the coordinates you need, click to pick the point. This method is fast and accurate. *See also* SNAP and DSETTINGS in Part II for details.

Well, I lied. Now AutoCAD has two kinds of snap. One I just described. The other is called polar snap. Right-click Snap on the status bar and choose Polar Snap On. Then right-click Snap again and click Settings. In the Drafting Settings dialog box, set the Polar Distance. Now when you draw or edit, AutoCAD creates a temporary alignment path but the SnapTip shows only your snap increments, such as .5000, 1.0000, 1.5000, and so on. Polar snap uses the angles that you set on the Polar Tracking tab of the same dialog box. *See also* DSETTINGS in Part II for details.

The itsy-bitsy, teeny-weeny, yellow polka-dot grid

Okay, so the grid isn't yellow; it's grayish. The grid is a rectangular array of dots that you can turn on to help you get your bearings. Usually, you want to set the grid equal to the snap. Click Grid on the status bar to turn the grid on. Right-click and choose Settings to set the grid size. *See also* GRID and DSETTINGS in Part II for further information.

For the squares among you: Drawing at right angles

Many things in life are at right angles. Walls and doors are at right angles from the floor (otherwise, the house comes tumbling down). The Ortho feature (*ortho* is Autospeak for *orthogonal*) enables you to draw at right angles only. Like snap, ortho (in the right situation) can increase drawing speed and accuracy. You can click Ortho on and off from the status bar. *See also* ORTHO and DSETTINGS in Part II.

Direct distance entry

Direct distance entry is a shortcut way to enter a polar coordinate. If you know the distance, move the cursor in the direction you want to go to indicate the angle and then type only the distance. Direct distance entry works best in orthogonal mode or with polar snap on because that way you can control the direction of the cursor. For example, to draw a line that is 6 units in the 90-degree direction, pick a start point and, at the To point: prompt, move the cursor in the 90-degree direction (up), type **6**, and press Enter.

Here's Lookin' at You, Kid

After you draw something, you often need to zoom in closer to see the fine detail of your masterpiece and then zoom out again to see the drawing as a whole. The ZOOM command has many helpful options. This command is indispensable, so be sure to look it up in Part II.

Real-time zoom enables you to zoom in and out as you move the cursor. Click Zoom Realtime on the Standard toolbar. Click and drag up to zoom in, or down to zoom out.

When you zoom in, you might find that you want to move a little to the right (or left, or whatever). *Panning* enables you to move from place to place in your drawing. You also can use the scroll bars to pan at right angles.

You can also do a real-time pan. Click Pan Realtime on the Standard toolbar. Then click and drag your drawing any way you want to go. Look up the PAN command in Part II.

If you have an IntelliMouse (the mouse with the little wheel on it), you can scroll the wheel to zoom in and out. You can also press the wheel and move the mouse around to pan.

The REDRAW and REGEN commands refresh the drawing screen. The REGEN command also recomputes coordinates, reindexes the database, and so on.

If you're drawing in 3D, you'll want to view your drawing from different angles. You can look at your 3D drawing from any angle, even from below. (I call that the gopher view.) On the menu, choose View⇨3D Views and choose Viewpoint Presets (the DDVPOINT command) or VPOINT on the submenu. These two commands offer two methods of specifying a viewpoint — choose the method that's most meaningful for you.

Two of the coolest new features of AutoCAD 2000 are persistent shading and 3D orbit. Persistent shading doesn't mean it's annoying, just that it continues until you turn it off. Don't you wish you could turn off persistent pests in your life so easily? Choose View⇨Shade and choose a submenu option. Choose the 2D Wireframe option to turn shading off and get back to "normalcy." You can draw and edit to your heart's content with shading on — it helps you visualize 3D models more easily. See the SHADEMODE command in Part II.

3D orbit lets you rotate your 3D model in any direction. You can even start a rotation and tell AutoCAD to keep on rotating the model on its own — you just sit back and watch! To start 3D Orbit, click 3D Orbit on the Standard toolbar. You'll find all the options by right-clicking. For more information, look for the 3DORBIT command in Part II.

Obviously, part of looking at your drawing involves plotting it. Look up the PLOT command for details and new features. You also might want to check out the concept of *layouts,* which is a way of setting up a drawing for plotting. Layouts are most useful for 3D drawings because they enable you to create floating viewports, each with a different view of your objects. But even 2D drawings can benefit from paper space. The procedure is a bit complex, but hey! — this is AutoCAD. Look up the following commands: LAYOUT, PSPACE, MSPACE, and MVIEW.

Be Choosy: Selecting Objects for Editing

No one ever drew a drawing without making a mistake. You always need to edit. Even the basic drawing process often involves copying or mirroring objects. Along with the editing process comes the need to select which objects to edit.

Which came first: Object or command?

When you want to make changes, you need to know two things: which command to use and which objects to change. Traditionally, AutoCAD required you to enter a command first and then select the objects. The Windows tradition, however, is to select objects first and then apply the command to those objects. Choose Tools⇨Options and click the Selection tab to customize the way you select objects.

AutoCAD, in true Autospeak, calls the concept of selecting the objects first and the command second *noun/verb selection.* You see, the object you're selecting is a thing, which is a *noun.* (You never thought of your circles as being nouns?) The command carries out an action, so it's a *verb.* The only good thing about all this nonsense is that if you choose Noun/Verb Selection (which you can do on the Selection tab of the Options dialog box — and it's the default anyway — you get the best of two worlds: AutoCAD accepts object selection first or second, whichever you want.

As an exercise in Autospeak, try turning your editing operations into little sentences, according to whether you select objects first or second. *I move a circle. A circle I move.* (I don't advise you to do this out loud if other people are around.)

Note that some commands don't accept object selection first, no matter what. Don't worry, if you try to select objects first with these commands and nothing happens, you'll soon figure it out.

You can use the SELECT command, which simply selects objects. Then you start a command and, at the `Select objects:` prompt, type **p**, which stands for *previous.* All the objects that you choose during the SELECT command are highlighted and ready for a little action.

Pick and click

When you choose an editing command, you usually see the `Select objects:` prompt. The crosshairs turn into a *pickbox,* which is a little box for picking objects. Move that box over the object that you want to pick, and then click.

Selection options

You can select objects in other ways, too. For example, you can create windows (or fences or polygons) around objects and then select everything inside the window. These methods are especially good for selecting many objects at the same time. All the objects that you have selected are called the *selection set.* **See also** the SELECT command for details.

Get a grip on yourself

Grips are little handles that you can use to select objects and choose a base point for an editing command. When you select an object, all the little handles appear, generally at strategic places such as endpoints and midpoints. Before you get too excited, you should know that the only tasks you can do with grips are stretch, move, copy, rotate, scale, and mirror.

Here's how to use grips. Select the object, using any selection method. Do *not* start a command. Then click the grip you want to use as the base point for the operation. It turns red (that's the default) and is now called a hot grip. Right-click to choose the operation you want from the cursor menu. If you need to specify a new point (for example, a new location for your grip), do so. In some operations, you can drag the grip. Each operation is slightly different, but the procedure is supposed to be intuitive, so play around. Command-line prompts appear, but the point is to manipulate the object using only the mouse. Press Esc once to remove the object from the selection set. Press Esc a second time to make the grips disappear.

Help!

Every once in a while, using AutoCAD makes you feel like you've been underwater for too long (you've forgotten to breathe), and you need someone to come rescue you. Sometimes, using Help really helps. Other times, well. . . .

Help comes in two species: regular and context sensitive. You get to regular help by choosing Help⇨AutoCAD Help. The command teleports you to the Help Contents screen, where you can choose the topic you need. Generally, you double-click either the Command Reference (for a list of commands) or the User's Guide (the user's manual). If you don't find the Contents screen helpful, click the Index tab. Try typing a topic or keyword to see what you get. If you don't get anything, you can scroll through the list and try to find what you want. When you find the topic, double-click it. Sometimes related topics appear in the Topics Found box. Double-click again to finally get the help you want.

Context-sensitive Help displays help on the command you're using. Start a command and press F1 (or type **'help** on the command line). The Help screen for that command appears. Dialog boxes also contain a Help button that provides help information for the dialog box. Many dialog boxes have a question mark in the upper-right corner. Click the question mark and click any item in the dialog box to get help related to that item.

Get Me Out of Here!

If you don't want to stay in AutoCAD forever (you could always draw a bed and go to sleep in your drawing), here's how to get out.

Use the QUIT command to exit. An even faster way to quit is to click the Close button (the little x at the top-right corner of your screen). Just to be extra safe, you should save your drawing first, but if you haven't saved all your changes, AutoCAD kindly prompts you to do so.

Part II

The Commands

Folks, here's the meat and potatoes of the book — a radical statement for a vegetarian like me! Each entry in this part tells you how to execute the command using the menus and the toolbars.

A note about those toolbars. When you first open AutoCAD, you probably see only four toolbars: the Standard toolbar along the top, the Object Properties toolbar underneath it, and the Draw and Modify toolbars. AutoCAD has many more toolbars, and you could be a bit mystified when I tell you to use the Solids toolbar and it's nowhere in sight. I humbly refer you to my explanation under the TOOLBAR command in this part, which explains how to pull toolbars out of a top hat. You can also right-click any toolbar and choose from a list of toolbars. Some toolbars have *flyouts,* which are just visual submenus. You click on a toolbar button, and out flies a bunch of buttons.

Under the "How to use it" sections that follow each command, I tell you how to use the command, walking you through the prompts or dialog box options. Then you usually find a section called "More stuff," which includes more advanced or unusual information as well as warnings, tips, and references.

In this part . . .

✔ **Using commands from 3D to A to Z**

✔ **Information about commands**

3D

Draws 3D polygon surfaces.

Toolbar: On the Surfaces toolbar, click the button of the shape you want to draw.

Menu: Choose Draw⇨Surfaces⇨3D Surfaces.

How to use it

If you use the menu, you get the 3D dialog box, but as soon as you choose a shape, AutoCAD throws you back to the lions, I mean, the command line. If you use the toolbar, you get a command-line prompt. In either case, you have the following options:

 First, specify one corner of the box and then a length and a width. Then type the height. Specify an angle for the rotation around the Z axis. If you use the Cube option, you only specify the length because the width is the same.

 Specify the center of the cone's base and then specify its radius or diameter. Then type the radius or diameter of the top. If you type 0 for the radius or diameter, you get a true cone; a bigger number results in a cone with its top chopped off. Now you type a height and the number of segments, that is, how many facets the cone has.`

 A dish is just the bottom half of a sphere. Specify the center, which is the center of the imaginary circle covering the top of the sphere. Then type a radius or a diameter. Now type the number of longitudinal segments around the sides of the bowl. Then type the number of latitudinal segments from the bottom of the bowl to its rim.

This is an upside-down dish. It works the same way as the Dish option.

 What's a 3D mesh? You'll see when you draw one. (I'm so helpful, aren't I?) It's easy. Just specify four corners — they can be anywhere in 3D space. Then type a Mesh M size between 2 and 256 (which in AutoCAD jargon means the number of row vertices) and a similar Mesh N size to specify the number of column vertices.

This command creates regular and truncated pyramids, ridges (like a pup tent), and tetrahedrons. Specify three base points. You can branch off into tetrahedron making (tetrahedrons have only three base points) and finish it with the apex, or continue bravely on and specify a fourth base point. Now, if you're making a pyramid, all you do is define the apex (which should be above the base) and you're finished. If you want a pup tent, choose the Ridge option and specify the two top ridge points. Finally, if you're making truncated shapes, choose the Top option and specify three or four top points, depending on the shape. AutoCAD prompts you as you go.

 To create a sphere, specify a center and radius or diameter and type a number of longitudinal and latitudinal segments as for a Dish.

 A torus is a 3D donut. Specify the center and then the radius or diameter of the torus. Then define the radius or diameter of the tube, which is the width or fatness of the donut. Finally, type a number of segments around the tube circumference and around the entire torus circumference. If you like your donuts squished flat, see the 2D DONUT command.

This is the shape of a triangular doorstop. It has one right angle. Specify the corner at the right angle, and type a length, width, and height. Finally, specify a rotation angle about the Z axis.

More stuff

Because these shapes are surfaces, they can be hidden, shaded, or rendered. *See also* HIDE, SHADEMODE, and RENDER.

3DARRAY

Creates 3D arrays.

Menu: Choose Modify⇨3D Operation⇨3D Array.

How to use it

Before you use this command, be sure that you know how to make plain-Jane 2D arrays. See the ARRAY command.

Select the objects to array. Pick either the Rectangular or Polar option. If you're making a rectangular array, type the number of rows, columns, and levels (levels is the third dimension). Finally, specify distances between the rows, columns, and levels.

To make a polar (circular) array, type the number of copies you want and the angle to fill, up to 360 degrees. Decide whether you want to rotate objects as they're copied (right-click and choose Yes or No). Now specify a center point for the array. The last prompt is a second point on the axis of rotation. These last two points create an imaginary axis about which the objects are arrayed.

3DFACE

Draws a 3D surface.

 Toolbar: Click the 3D Face button on the Surfaces toolbar.

Menu: Choose Draw⇨Surfaces⇨3D Face.

How to use it

3DFACE creates surfaces in 3D space. You simply specify X,Y,Z coordinates for each point, moving clockwise or counterclockwise. AutoCAD prompts you for the first through fourth points and then continues to prompt you for the third and fourth points so that you can continue to create adjacent faces. Press Enter to end the command.

3DFACE is not an easy way to create surfaces because you have to know the coordinates of each point, but it can be very useful for creating odd-looking surfaces.

More stuff

Before you specify any point, you can type **i** at the command line to make the edge created by that point and the next point invisible. This process creates realistic looking models because it creates complex shapes with no internal edge lines.

The EDGE command controls and edits the visibility of 3DFACE edges.

3DORBIT

Enables you to rotate your 3D model so you can see it from any angle.

 Toolbar: Click the 3D Orbit button on the Standard toolbar.

Menu: Choose View➪3D Orbit.

How to use it

AutoCAD displays the *arcball.* You have three main types of rotation:

+ If you click and drag your cursor outside the arcball, your model turns round and round like a top.

+ If you click and drag your cursor inside the arcball, your model moves in the direction you drag.

+ If you click and drag one of the little circles, the models rotates around the arcball's axis — its vertical axis if you drag from the left or right circle or its horizontal axis if you drag from the top or bottom circle.

Absolutely the coolest feature is continuous orbit, which rotates your model on its own, while you watch. In 3D orbit, right-click and choose More➪Continuous Orbit. Then click and drag your model in the direction you want it to rotate and let go. Don't get hypnotized!

To get back to your starting view, right-click and choose Reset View.

More stuff

Other options available by right-clicking are pan, zoom, zoom window, zoom extents, and preset views. You can also choose between parallel (the default) and perspective views (right-click and choose Perspective).

You can set front and back clipping planes that block your view outside the planes. Use clipping planes when something blocks your view. In 3D orbit, right-click and choose More⇨Adjust Clipping Planes. AutoCAD opens a special window that rotates your model 90 degrees so you can drag the front and back clipping planes into place.

See also CAMERA to change the start and end points of the view. You can view your model in 3D orbit with shading on — see SHADE-MODE.

3DPOLY

Draws a polyline in 3D space — lines only, no arcs.

Menu: Choose Draw⇨3D Polyline.

How to use it

AutoCAD starts with the Specify start point of polyline: prompt. When you specify the point (using X,Y,Z coordinates), AutoCAD asks you for the endpoint. AutoCAD continues to ask you for the endpoint of segments, and you keep on providing coordinates until you press Enter to complete the command.

The only other options are Undo (for those few of us who may make a mistake specifying those 3D points) and Close, which draws a line from the last endpoint to the first point.

More stuff

The PEDIT command edits 3D polylines.

ADCENTER

Gives you access to other drawings and drawing components such as blocks (sometimes called symbols), linetypes, layouts, text styles, dimension styles, xrefs, and raster images so you can insert them in your drawing.

Toolbar: Click the AutoCAD DesignCenter button on the Standard toolbar.

Menu: Choose Tools➪AutoCAD DesignCenter.

How to use it

The DesignCenter has its own toolbar. Click Tree View Toggle to turn on and off the tree view, which is like Windows Explorer. Use this to find the drawing that has the components you want. The Open Drawings button lets you see only currently open drawings.

Click the plus sign next to the drawing to see what types of components it contains. Click the one you want, such as Blocks. All the blocks in the drawing are displayed in the right pane. To insert any component into your drawing, drag it onto the drawing area.

More stuff

Click Favorites on the DesignCenter toolbar to quickly get to components of drawings that you've saved in the Favorites folder. Click Preview to see a preview of blocks and drawings.

You can adjust the size of the entire DesignCenter or each pane by placing the cursor over the border, clicking, and dragging. By default, the DesignCenter is docked but you can undock it. Ctrl+2 is the secret code for both displaying and closing the DesignCenter.

ALIGN

Aligns objects with other objects.

Menu: Choose Modify➪3D Operation➪Align.

How to use it

First, don't let the 3D Operation menu item scare you. Align works nicely for 2D drawing as well. AutoCAD prompts you to select the objects that you want to move. These objects are called *source objects.* You can specify one, two, or three pairs of points.

Aligning using one pair of points is just like using the MOVE command. AutoCAD prompts you for the first source point and the first destination point. Your first source point might be a corner of the rectangle you want to move. Your first destination point might be the midpoint of a line. The corner of the rectangle moves to the midpoint of the line. When AutoCAD prompts you for the second source point, press Enter to complete the command.

When you use two pairs of points, you can both move and rotate the first object to match the position and angle of the second object. Start in the same way as you do for one-point alignment, but then pick a second source point and a second destination point. Press Enter when prompted for a third source point. AutoCAD asks whether you want to scale the object. Choose Yes to scale the source object relative to your destination point. AutoCAD moves the first object and rotates it so that the imaginary line created by your two source points matches up with the imaginary line created by your two destination points.

Using three pairs of points allows a second rotation of the object in a different direction and is used for only 3D objects. Specify three pairs of source and destination points. AutoCAD not only moves and rotates the first object to match up the first two pairs of points but also tumbles the object so that the third pair of points is aligned.

APERTURE

Changes the size of the *aperture,* which is the object snap target box. *See also* the OPTIONS command.

ARC

Draws an arc.

 Toolbar: Click the Arc button on the Draw toolbar.

Menu: Choose Draw⇨Arc.

How to use it

AutoCAD gives you a dizzying array of options, but the concept is simple. First, choose Start point or Center and specify that point. (You can also press Enter to start your arc at a point that is tangent to the last line or arc you drew.)

AutoCAD then prompts you with your next options and guides you through the creation of your arc. You decide which points you want to specify and in what order. The elements of the arc (depending on your choices) are Start point, End point, Second point, Center, included Angle, Length of chord, and Radius.

More stuff

See Chapter 7 of *AutoCAD 2000 For Dummies* for more on arcs.

AREA

Calculates the area and perimeter of an object or an area you specify.

 Toolbar: On the Object Properties toolbar, click Inquiry and then click Area.

Menu: Choose Tools⇨Inquiry⇨Area.

How to use it

Your options are First point, Object, Add, and Subtract. If you want the area and perimeter of a 2D closed object, choose Object and then select the object. Select the first point to define an area by selecting points. AutoCAD prompts you for additional points. Add and Subtract enable you to add objects or points until you have the shape you want. Press Enter to complete the command.

ARRAY

Creates copies of an object in a rectangular or polar (that is, circular) pattern.

Toolbar: Click the Array button on the Modify toolbar.

Menu: Choose Modify⇨Array.

How to use it

Select the object or objects you want to copy. Rectangular gives you copies in rows and columns. Tell AutoCAD how many rows and columns you want. Then type the distance between the rows and columns. (You can also point to diagonal corners of an imaginary rectangle. The rectangle's width and height define the distance between the columns and rows, respectively.) Positive distances build the array up and to the right. Negative distances build it down and to the left.

Select Polar to array copies around a center point. AutoCAD prompts you for the Center point, number of items, and angle to fill (360 degrees fills a circle). You have to specify only two of the three prompts. Press Enter to pass by the prompt you don't want. Finally, tell AutoCAD whether you want to rotate the objects as they're copied.

ATTDEF

Defines an attribute, which is text usually attached to a block.

Menu: Choose Draw⇨Block⇨Define Attributes.

How to use it

Attributes can be used just to facilitate the entry of text labels related to blocks, but they also enable you to extract all the information in a database. The entire process of creating and inserting blocks with attributes includes four steps:

1. **Create the object(s).** You can turn the objects into a block later.

2. **Define the attribute using ATTDEF.** You probably want to put the attribute next to the block. You can define more than one attribute for a block.

3. **Create the block, including in it both the object(s) and the attribute(s).** When you select the attributes as part of creating the block, select them individually in the order in which you want AutoCAD to prompt you.

4. **Insert the block.** AutoCAD prompts you for the attribute information.

ATTDEF opens the Attribute Definition dialog box, where you define the attributes.

Mode: You can choose to make the attribute invisible; give it a constant value; force verification of each attribute; and create a preset default.

Attribute: Specify a tag, which is the name of the attribute. No spaces allowed. Specify a prompt, which you see when you insert the attribute values. Prompts can have spaces. If you specified a preset default, type the value here.

Insertion Point: You can type X,Y,Z coordinates or click Pick Point to pick a point in the drawing. As soon as you do, the dialog box magically returns.

Text Options: Specify the justification, style, height, and rotation of the text, as with the text commands. If you're creating more than one attribute and like to be neat, you can click the Align below previous attribute button to put the attribute directly below the previous one. Click OK to complete the command.

More stuff

If you make a mistake defining your attribute and catch it before you've defined the block, use DDEDIT. After you insert the block and type the specific attribute data, use ATTEDIT to change the data.

See also the DTEXT and STYLE commands for information on setting the text options, and the BLOCK and INSERT commands for information on creating and inserting blocks.

The ATTDIA system variable determines whether AutoCAD uses a dialog box to prompt you for attribute values when you insert a block with attributes. See Part III. When you use a dialog box, the Verify and Preset modes have no significance.

ATTDISP

Sets the visibility of all attributes in a drawing. An *attribute* is explanatory text attached to a block.

Menu: Choose View⇨Display⇨Attribute Display.

How to use it

When you create an attribute using ATTDEF, you decide whether or not it will be visible. This command overrides that decision. AutoCAD gives you three options: Normal (leaves your original decision alone), ON (makes all attributes visible), and OFF (makes all attributes invisible).

ATTEDIT

Changes attribute information and definitions.

Menu: Choose Modify⇨Attribute⇨Single *or* Global.

How to use it

This command enables you to edit attributes individually, one by one, or to make global changes to all of them at the same time. At the prompt Edit attributes one at a time? [Yes/No] ⟨Y⟩: type **y** to be prompted for each attribute individually and **n** to edit globally. Then AutoCAD prompts you for the name of the block, the attribute tag, and the attribute value, so that you can edit all copies of it.

ATTEXT 35

Then you select an attribute and get the following options:

Value	Changes or replaces the value of the attribute. Use Change to change a string of characters instead of replacing the entire value.
Position	Changes the text insertion point.
Height	Changes the text height.
Angle	Changes the rotation angle of the text.
Style	Changes the text style.
Layer	Changes the layer.
Color	Changes the color.

More stuff

ATTDEF creates an attribute.

ATTEXT

Extracts attribute data to a file for use as a database.

Command line only

How to use it

Now comes the fun stuff, extracting your attribute data into a file for use in a database program. But it ain't easy. Remember, you're using the feared and awesome AutoCAD.

First, you have to make a template file. This is a plain text file that AutoCAD uses to design the database. You can use Notepad, which comes with Windows. (Choose Start⇨Programs⇨Accessories⇨ Notepad.)

Suppose you have a block named DESK that contains two attributes — name and phone number. You want to extract the block name, its X and Y coordinates, and the name and phone number attributes. Your kid's teacher uses these attributes to make up a class layout of which student sits where and wants to extract the information to make up a phone tree using each student's name and phone number.

The attribute file you create in the text editor should look something like the following figure.

```
ADQR2-01TIF.txt - Notepad
File  Edit  Search  Help
BL:NAME        C010000
BL:X           N006000
BL:Y           N006000
SPACESAVER     C002000
NAME           C015000
PHONE          C008000
```

AutoCAD is finicky about templates. (Oh, for a Template File wizard!) As you type, end each line, including the last, by pressing Enter. To separate each field, use spaces, not tabs.

After you create the template file, save it and remember its name. (Better yet, write down the name.) Then go into the ATTEXT command, which opens up the Attribute Extraction dialog box.

First, select the format you want for the file you're creating. Usually, you use a comma-delimited file, which means that commas appear between the fields of each record, or a space-delimited file (you can guess what that means). The fields of space-delimited files have a fixed width. Which to use? That depends on the database application you're going to use. The secret is to go to the documentation of that program and find out what types of files it can import.

Now click Select Objects. This action returns you to your drawing so that you can select the blocks with the attributes that you want in the database. When you're finished, the Attribute Extraction dialog box returns.

Next to the Template File button, type the name of your template file. (You wrote it down, remember?) If you click Template File, you get a dialog box (similar to a File⇨Open box) that enables you to select the file from a list.

Next to Output File, type a name for the database file you want to create. AutoCAD automatically gives it a *.TXT* file extension. You can also navigate through folders to find the proper location.

Finally, click OK to extract the attribute information and create the database file. Here is the result.

```
Class List.txt - Notepad                          _ □ X
File  Edit  Search  Help
DESK        6    3    Acey          469-8382
DESK        6    5    Eliyah        472-9348
DESK        3    5    Yeshayah      469-1832
DESK        3    3    Jeremy        472-9780
```

The name of the block (DESK) and the X and Y coordinates are a bit useless, but they're the standard options available with ATTEXT. (If your kid's teacher needs X,Y coordinates to find your kid, you'd better consider switching schools!) If you want, you can import the database file into a database or spreadsheet program. There, you can manipulate your data to your heart's content.

More stuff

AutoCAD can also connect you directly to an outside database. I left that stuff out (it's a book in itself).

ATTREDEF

Redefines a block with attached attributes and updates the attributes according to the new definition.

Command line only

How to use it

First, explode one copy of the block if you want to change its parts. ATTREDEF prompts you for the name of the block you want to redefine. Then you select the objects for the block, including the attributes. When AutoCAD prompts you for an insertion base point, pick the same point you chose when you created the block. AutoCAD updates the block and its attributes wherever the block has been inserted.

AUDIT

Finds errors in the drawing caused by data storage malfunctions.

Menu: Choose File⇨Drawing Utilities⇨Audit.

How to use it

AutoCAD asks permission to correct any detected errors. Choose Yes or No.

More stuff

The RECOVER command tries to retrieve those really messed up drawings that you can't even open.

BACKGROUND

Defines the background, such as a tree or a colored pattern, for a rendered 3D scene.

 Toolbar: Click the Background button on the Render toolbar.

Menu: Choose View⇨Render⇨Background.

How to use it

Choose the type of background: solid color, gradient (a graded blend of colors), image (from a graphic file), or merge (to combine your rendering with your current screen image).

Your next step depends on what type of background you chose. For example, if you chose solid, you can select a color. If you chose gradient, you get controls to choose the colors and how they blend. If you chose image, use the Image section to choose a graphic file.

More stuff

Click Preview to see what your background will look like after you create the rendering. *See also* RENDER.

BASE

Sets the insertion base point for your drawing.

Menu: Choose Draw⇨Block⇨Base.

How to use it

If you want to change the base point, simply specify the point.

More stuff

 Use this command when you plan to insert the drawing into another drawing and want to reference a point on an object. Otherwise, the base point should generally be (0,0,0).

BHATCH

Creates a hatch pattern inside an enclosed area. A hatch pattern isn't an instinct of baby birds. It's just a bunch of parallel lines (or similar patterns) that fill in an object or enclosed area. This command enables you to create an *associative* hatch pattern; the hatch pattern is adjusted automatically if you change the enclosed area.

You can also use a solid fill to fill in an area.

Toolbar: Click the Hatch button on the Draw toolbar.

Menu: Choose Draw⇨Hatch.

How to use it

The Boundary Hatch dialog box opens with the Quick tab on top. Here are your options:

Type	Enables you to choose a Predefined hatch pattern (the ones AutoCAD gives you), a User-defined pattern that enables you to define a hatch out of the current linetype, or a custom hatch pattern you've created.
Pattern	Selects your hatch pattern from AutoCAD's predefined list.
Custom	If you selected a Custom hatch Type, enables you to choose a custom pattern.
Angle	Rotates the pattern relative to the X axis (but some patterns are created at an angle, so specifying an angle can create unintended results).
Scale	Increases or decreases the size of a hatch pattern.
Spacing	If you selected a User-defined hatch Type, defines how wide apart the lines are.

If you're creating a user-defined hatch, you can check Double to create a second set of lines 90 degrees from the first set. By default, hatches are *associative,* meaning that they resize themselves if you resize their boundary. If you don't want this nice feature, click Nonassociative.

After you have defined the hatch, you tell AutoCAD where to put it. Click Pick Points to pick points inside closed boundaries that your objects create. Click Select Objects to select objects that contain closed boundaries (such as circles and closed polylines).

Before you complete the command, click Preview to preview your hatch — a wise idea. The dialog box disappears, and you see what damage you've brought about. Continue gets you back to the dialog box. Click OK to create the hatch.

To make things easier, you can specify a hatch you've already created and copy its pattern type and properties to your new hatch. Click Inherit Properties (don't expect to find that your rich uncle has left you a major hotel chain), and AutoCAD prompts you to select the original hatch.

More stuff

Click the Advanced tab, if you're the daring type, to define how objects within objects (islands) are hatched. As you select each hatching style, an image tile shows you an example. Another useful option is Retain Boundaries. If not selected, you get just the hatch without boundaries around it.

 See Chapter 11 in *AutoCAD 2000 For Dummies* for more on hatching.

BLOCK

Creates one named object from a group of objects, called a *block*. The block can then be inserted elsewhere using the INSERT command.

Toolbar: Click the Make Block button on the Draw toolbar.

Menu: Choose Draw➪Block➪Make.

How to use it

Type a name for your block in the Name box of the Block Definition dialog box. Click Select Objects to return to your drawing and select the objects for the block. When you end object selection, you return to the dialog box. In the Base Point section, click Pick Point to choose a base point or type coordinates. When you insert the block, the base point of the block is placed at the insertion point you specify in your drawing.

 Use an object snap to create an exact insertion base point. The lower-left corner or center of your block are good choices.

Click Retain Objects to keep the objects you used to create the block. Click Delete to delete the objects — your objects disappear when you make the block! Uh oh! Just type OOPS on the command line to bring them back. Click Convert to Block to convert the objects to the block you just defined.

 Your block name can have spaces and be up to 255 characters.

BOX **41**

More stuff

See also INSERT, EXPLODE, and WBLOCK for more on blocks. You can also check out Chapter 14 in *AutoCAD 2000 For Dummies.*

BOUNDARY

Creates a closed region or polyline from an object or from the intersection of objects that form an enclosed area.

Menu: Choose Draw⇨Boundary.

How to use it

The Boundary Creation dialog box appears with the following options:

Object Type	Choose either Region or Polyline.
Boundary Set	By default, AutoCAD analyzes everything — you do nothing (the easiest option!). Click New to select objects, restricting AutoCAD to a smaller boundary set for quicker results, especially if you have a complex drawing.
Pick Points	AutoCAD prompts you to select an internal point. You pick a point or points inside objects to define the boundary. Press Enter to end the selection of points and create the boundary.

More stuff

See also the PLINE and REGION commands for more information.

BOX

Draws a 3D solid box.

Toolbar: Click the Box button on the Solids toolbar.

Menu: Choose Draw⇨Solids⇨Box.

How to use it

The first prompt offers you the choice of defining the box from its center or from a corner. If you choose the corner method (the default), specify a point on the base of the box. Now you have three options:

Other corner	Specify the diagonally opposite corner of the base of the box. AutoCAD then prompts you for a height. A positive number makes the box rise along the positive Z axis. (A negative number makes the box descend into the nether regions — in the direction of the negative Z axis.)
Length	Right-click and choose Length. AutoCAD prompts you for a length, a width, and then a height. Positive numbers expand the box along positive axes. (Negative numbers expand the box in the direction of the negative Z axis.)
Cube	Type **c** to draw a cube. Specify a length, and AutoCAD figures out that the rest of the sides are the same and draws your cube.

The center option enables you to specify the center of the box instead of the first corner. All the other prompts are the same.

BREAK

Creates a break in an object.

Toolbar: Click the Break button on the Modify toolbar.

Menu: Choose Modify⇨Break.

How to use it

You can do this command in two ways:

+ First, select the object to break by clicking it any old place. Then right-click and choose First Point and specify your first point. Then specify your second point. AutoCAD erases the object between the two points. If the second point is beyond the end of your object, AutoCAD erases the object from your first point to its end.

+ If you're the precise type, you can select the object in a location that's also the first point you want to select. Then select the second break point, and you're finished.

More stuff

You can break lines, arcs, polylines, circles, ellipses, donuts, and so on. To break an object into two parts with no gap, type @ for the second point. The object still looks like it's one object but it's actually two.

BROWSER

Opens your Internet browser according to your system's default settings.

Toolbar: Click the Launch Browser button on the Web toolbar.

How to use it

AutoCAD prompts you for a URL address and then opens your Web browser and connects you to the location. Of course, you still have to enter any required passwords and such. By the way, you need either Netscape Navigator 3.0 (or later) or Microsoft Internet Explorer 3.0 (or later) for this command to work, as well as an active Internet connection.

More stuff

You can open drawings from the Web or any URL (including an intranet) by simply typing the URL in the Open dialog box. You can also save to any URL in the Save Drawing dialog box.

'CAL

Evaluates expressions as you draw through the use of an online geometry calculator.

Command line only

How to use it

 This calculator is loaded with features not easily explained in a Quick Reference book. It can calculate regular numeric expressions, as well as work with vectors (lines or any distance and direction), measurements (feet and inches), angles, and more. You can use snap modes in your expressions.

Here are two simple examples:

+ Start the **CAL** command. When AutoCAD prompts you for an expression, type something like **(575+72.2154) * (2^5) – (6 * PI)**. In other words, something you'd never figure out yourself in a million years. (I got 20692.0, did you?)

+ Suppose you want to move a circle so that its center is halfway between the midpoint of two lines. Type **move** on the command line and select the circle. When AutoCAD prompts you for a base point, type **cen** and select the circle. At the Second point of displacement prompt, type **'cal** (to use it as a transparent command). AutoCAD asks for an expression. Type **(mid+mid)/2**. AutoCAD then wants to know which mid-points you're talking about and prompts you to select an object for each midpoint snap. Select one line and then the other. AutoCAD moves the circle. Cool!

CAMERA

Defines the viewer's point and target point for 3D views.

 Toolbar: Click the Camera button on the View toolbar (which is also a flyout on the Standard toolbar).

How to use it

At the first prompt, specify the new camera position. The camera position is where you are standing, so to speak. At the second prompt, specify the new target, that is, where you are looking. Set up a view (using VPOINT or DDVPOINT) so you can easily see both the camera and target points.

More stuff

Use this before the 3DORBIT command to define the viewpoint of your 3D view.

CHAMFER

Bevels (cuts at an angle) two intersecting lines (or almost intersecting lines).

Toolbar: Click the Chamfer button on the Modify toolbar.

Menu: Choose Modify⇨Chamfer.

How to use it

At the prompt, first define the distances, or angle, or both. Then repeat the command, select the first line, select the second line, and — presto! — AutoCAD creates a new line at an angle to the original lines. Here are the options:

Polyline	Chamfers an entire polyline (every angle).
Distance	Specifies how far from the intersection the chamfer starts. The first distance affects the first line you select and the second distance affects the second line you select. By default, both distances are equal to create a symmetrical chamfer.
Angle	Defines the chamfer by a distance from the first line and an angle to the second line.
Trim	Trims the two selected lines so that they meet the chamfer, but you can nix that.
Method	Tells AutoCAD whether to use the Distance or Angle method of defining a chamfer.

More stuff

You can also chamfer a 3D solid. *See also* the FILLET command.

CHANGE

Changes certain properties of existing objects.

Command line only

How to use it

Select the objects. The first option is Change point. For a line, you pick a new endpoint, and AutoCAD changes the line's endpoint. (If ORTHO is on, you'll get odd results!) For more than one line, AutoCAD moves all the endpoints to the change point. For a circle, you specify a point that defines the new radius. For text, the point you select becomes the new text insertion point. For blocks, the point becomes the new insertion base point. If you select text and press Enter at the `Change point:` prompt, AutoCAD prompts you to change the text's properties.

The second option is Properties. *See also* the CHPROP command.

More stuff

This command might give you unpredictable results if you select lines with other types of objects, so use CHANGE on one type of object at a time. The PROPERTIES command enables you to change properties of objects.

CHPROP

Changes an existing object's properties: color, layer, linetype, lineweight, and if appropriate (that means if Ann Landers approves), linetype scale and thickness.

Command line only

How to use it

Select the objects you want to change. Then right-click and choose one of the following options.

Color	See the COLOR command.
Layer	See the LAYER command.
Linetype	See the LINETYPE command.
Linetype Scale	See the LTSCALE command.
Lineweight	Type the lineweight you want. (Remember that the LWT button must appear pressed in on the status bar to show lineweights.)
Thickness	Type the thickness you want.

Press Enter to end the command, or right-click and choose another option.

More stuff

You can also change the layer of an object by selecting it, clicking the Layer Control drop-down list from the Object Properties toolbar, and choosing a new layer. The Object Properties toolbar also has Color Control, Linetype Control, and Lineweight Control drop-down lists so that you can change an object's color, linetype, and lineweight, respectively.

See also the COLOR, LAYER, LINETYPE, LTSCALE, and ELEV commands.

CIRCLE

Draws a circle.

 Toolbar: Click the Circle button on the Draw toolbar.

Menu: Choose Draw⇨Circle.

How to use it

You have four ways to define a circle:

Center Point	Pick the center point. Then pick a radius or type a length. Or type d (for diameter) and pick the diameter or type its length.
3P	This isn't the beginning of 3PO's name. (Remember *Star Wars?*) It stands for 3 points. Specify three points on the circumference of the circle.
2P	Specify two opposing points on the circumference of the circle.
TTR	It means Tangent, Tangent, Radius. You need two other objects nearby for the circle to be tangent to. Select the two objects and then type a radius length. AutoCAD sometimes gives unexpected results because more than one circle can meet your definition or because a circle can't fit with the specifications you gave

CLOSE

Closes the current drawing.

Menu: Choose File⇨Close.

You can also click the drawing's Close button at the top right of the screen (just below the application's Close button).

How to use it

Now that you can finally open more than one drawing, you need a way to close drawings without closing AutoCAD. CLOSE is that way.

If you have made changes to the drawing, AutoCAD reminds you to save them, never fear.

COLOR

Sets the color for new objects.

Toolbar: On the Object Properties toolbar, use the Color Control drop-down list and choose a color with no object selected.

Menu: Choose Format⇨Color.

How to use it

This command opens the Select Color dialog box, opening a vista of color possibilities. You can select one of the standard colors or select from the full color palette. You can also select BYLAYER, which gives new objects the color assigned to their layer (the default), or BYBLOCK, which draws new objects in the default color until they're grouped into a block. The inserted block takes on the block's color setting.

More stuff

When you define a layer, you include a color. Generally, the best way to use color is to simply change the layer. Think twice before changing the color of objects using COLOR because this change overrides the layer color definition. If objects are on the same layer but have different colors, expect to be confused! See the LAYER command.

CONE

Draws a solid cone.

 Toolbar: Click the Cone button on the Solids toolbar.

Menu: Choose Draw⇨Solids⇨Cone.

How to use it

The default is to create a cone with a circular base. Specify the center point of the base. You can then specify the radius, or right-click and choose Diameter to specify the diameter. At the next prompt, type a height. (A negative height draws an upside-down cone, like an ice cream cone.) Or you can right-click and choose Apex and specify a point for the apex. Use the apex option if you want to tip the entire cone at an angle (the Leaning Tower of Pisa look).

If you choose the elliptical option at the first prompt, you define an ellipse just as for the ELLIPSE command, using either the axis or the center method. The rest of the prompts are the same.

COPY

Copies objects.

 Toolbar: Click the Copy button on the Modify toolbar.

Menu: Choose Modify⇨Copy.

How to use it

Select the object or objects that you want to copy and press Enter to complete the selection process. AutoCAD responds with the `Specify base point or displacement, or [Multiple]:` prompt.

To move using the base point method, specify a point as the location to copy from. The point is often on the object(s) you're copying. AutoCAD then prompts you for a second point of displacement that shows the distance and location from the base point. You can pick a point, use an object snap, or type a coordinate, such as @@min2,0.

To move using the displacement method, type the displacement without the @, as in @min2,0 and press Enter. At the next prompt, press Enter.

More stuff

You can right-click and choose Multiple, and AutoCAD continues to prompt you for second points so that you can make as many copies as you want. Press Enter to complete the command.

COPYBASE

Copies objects to the Windows clipboard with a base point so you can paste them precisely.

Menu: Choose Edit⇨Copy with Base Point.

Shortcut menu: Right-click in the drawing area and choose Copy with Base Point.

How to use it

Specify the base point; then select the object or objects. Or select the objects first and then start the command. *See also* PASTECLIP.

COPYCLIP

Copies objects to the Windows clipboard.

Toolbar: Click the Copy button on the Standard toolbar.

Menu: Choose Edit⇨Copy.

Shortcut menu: Right-click in the drawing area and choose Copy.

How to use it

Select objects, either before or after starting the command. *See also* PASTECLIP.

CUTCLIP

Moves objects to the Windows clipboard.

Toolbar: Click the Cut button on the Standard toolbar.

Menu: Choose Edit⇨Cut.

Shortcut menu: Right-click in the drawing area and choose Cut.

How to use it

Select objects, either before or after starting the command. *See also* PASTECLIP.

CYLINDER

Draws a solid cylinder.

 Toolbar: Click the Cylinder button on the Solids toolbar.

Menu: Choose Draw⇨Solids⇨Cylinder.

How to use it

If you want the base of your cylinder to be a circle, the procedure is easy. Specify the center point of the base circle. Type the radius or the diameter. Radius is the default, but you can right-click and choose Diameter. Now AutoCAD prompts you to type the height but gives you an option to specify the center of the other end of the cylinder. Either task completes the command.

If you want the base of your cylinder to be an ellipse, choose the Elliptical option. AutoCAD prompts you to define the ellipse. The rest is the same as the circular cylinder, defining either the height or the center of the other end.

More stuff

You can also draw a circle or ellipse and EXTRUDE it. *See also* the ELLIPSE command.

How to use it

AutoCAD displays information about every object in the drawing — lots of it. Press Enter to continue from page to page. Press Esc to cancel.

DDEDIT

Edits text and attributes.

 Toolbar: Click the Edit Text button on the Modify II toolbar.

Menu: Choose Modify⇨Text.

Shortcut menu: After selecting text, right-click in the drawing area, and choose Mtext Edit or Text Edit (depending on the type of text you selected).

How to use it

Select the text to edit. What happens next depends on how you created the text. If you used the TEXT or DTEXT command, AutoCAD opens the Edit Text dialog box. If you used MTEXT to create paragraph text, AutoCAD opens the Multiline Text Editor. From then on, editing the text is straightforward. Click OK to close the dialog box or text editor, and then press Enter to end the command.

More stuff

You can also edit attribute text with this command, but you have to explode the block first. AutoCAD opens the Edit Attribute Definition dialog box, enabling you to change the tag, prompt, and default value.

DDPTYPE

Defines how points are displayed.

Menu: Choose Format⇨Point Style.

How to use it

The Point Style dialog box opens. Click on the picture of the style you want. Type the point size. If you want the points to look the same on your screen no matter how much you zoom in or out, click Set Size Relative to Screen. Use this command before creating points with the POINT command.

DDVPOINT

Controls the 3D angle from which you view your drawing.

Menu: Choose View⇨3D Views⇨Viewpoint Presets.

How to use it

AutoCAD opens the Viewpoint Presets dialog box. First, click Absolute to WCS, which calculates relative to the plan view and is easiest to comprehend. However, if you like to get esoteric and are already in some other UCS (user coordinate system), go ahead and click Relative to UCS.

If this is your first time using this command, it probably won't be clear until you play around with it and see the results in your drawing.

Imagine that you're Superman, flying around the Earth. In an instant, you can see the Earth from any viewpoint you choose. Now fly down to Earth and create a viewpoint.

On the left is a square with angles marked about a circle. This is where you define your viewing angle relative to the X axis while remaining in the XY plane (otherwise known as Flatland). Click inside the circle to specify any degree, or click outside the circle to specify degrees in the increments shown. Or type the degrees you want in the X Axis text box.

Because 0 is the X axis, if you choose a 45-degree angle, you'll be looking at your 3D object from halfway between its right side and its back side.

Now go to the right side of the dialog box to define your viewing angle relative to the XY plane, which means going up or down in the Z direction. Again you can click the inside for an exact angle, click the outside for the increments shown, or type the degree you want in the XY Plane text box. If you choose a 30-degree angle, you'll be looking at your 3D object from 30 degrees above your object.

Click OK to return to your drawing and see the results. Try DDVPOINT with many different angles until you get the hang of it.

The great thing about this dialog box is the panic button in the middle called Set to Plan View. When you get totally befuddled, click this button to return to 2D space. Ahh, that looks familiar!

More stuff

VPOINT accomplishes the same thing on the command line using a different system, called the compass-and-axis tripod. You can also enter X,Y,Z coordinates. *See also* 3DORBIT.

See Chapter 15 of *AutoCAD 2000 For Dummies.*

DIMALIGNED

Draws an aligned linear dimension. When a line is at an angle, an aligned dimension is drawn parallel to the line.

Toolbar: Click the Aligned Dimension button on the Dimension toolbar.

Menu: Choose Dimension⇨Aligned.

How to use it

You can press Enter and just select an object to dimension. Then AutoCAD automatically creates the extension lines that extend from the object to the dimension line. If you don't like AutoCAD's way of doing things, you can instead pick an origin for the first extension line, and AutoCAD prompts you for the second point.

Next, AutoCAD asks you to specify where you want the dimension line and offers Text, Mtext, and Angle options. If you specify the location for the dimension command, AutoCAD creates the dimension and ends the command. If you choose an option, answer the option prompts. AutoCAD then prompts you again for the dimension line location, which you specify to complete the command.

Text enables you to use the command line to customize the text. Mtext opens the Multiline Text Editor. In the Text Editor, you see brackets that represent the dimension text that AutoCAD thinks you want. You can keep it and add your own text before or after the brackets or delete the brackets and insert your own text. Angle sets the angle of the text.

 When you delete the brackets, you lose *associativity*. That means the dimension measurement is not automatically adjusted if you change the size of the object being dimensioned.

More stuff

 Remember that the appearance of your dimension is controlled by the DIMSTYLE command. Chapter 10 in *AutoCAD 2000 For Dummies* has more on dimensioning.

DIMANGULAR

Draws an angular dimension that measures an angle.

 Toolbar: Click the Angular Dimension button on the Dimension toolbar.

Menu: Choose Dimension⇨Angular.

How to use it

AutoCAD prompts you to select an arc, a circle, a line. You can also press Enter.

If you press Enter, AutoCAD prompts you for three points that define a vertex and two endpoints. This prompt is for measuring an angle that you create on the fly.

If you select an arc, AutoCAD uses the arc's center as the vertex and measures the angle from the arc's start point to its endpoint.

If you select a circle, you need to tell AutoCAD what part of the circle you want to dimension. The point on which you selected the circle is used as the start of the dimension, so watch where you're pointing! AutoCAD prompts you for a second point. The circle's center is the angle's vertex.

You can even select a line, and AutoCAD asks for a second line that must be at an angle to the first.

After you've finished telling AutoCAD what to dimension, the dimension line location prompt appears with the Mtext/Text/Angle options. If you specify the location for the dimension command, AutoCAD creates the dimension and ends the command.

The Text option enables you to customize the text on the command line. Mtext opens the Multiline Text Editor. In the Text Editor, you see brackets, which represent the dimension text that AutoCAD thinks you want. You can keep it and add your own text before or after the brackets or delete the brackets and insert your own text. Angle changes the angle of the dimension text.

When you delete the brackets, you lose *associativity.* That means the dimension measurement is not automatically adjusted if you change the size of the object being dimensioned,.

DIMBASELINE

Draws a linear, angular, or ordinate dimension that continues from the beginning of the previous (or a selected) dimension. This means that the second dimension includes the first and the second measurements, the third includes all three measurements, and so on.

Toolbar: Click the Baseline Dimension on the Dimension toolbar.

Menu: Choose Dimension⮒Baseline.

How to use it

If the previous dimension was linear, angular, or ordinate, AutoCAD assumes that you want to continue working from that dimension and enables you to simply specify the beginning of the second dimension's extension line. AutoCAD keeps asking the same question over and over so that you can continue to dimension, until you press Esc.

Or you can press Enter to select a dimension to start with and continue from there. To start from scratch, you first create a regular dimension. Then you can use this command.

DIMCENTER

Draws a center mark or line through the center of a circle or an arc.

 Toolbar: From the Dimension toolbar, click the Center Mark button.

Menu: Choose Dimension⇨Center Mark.

How to use it

 All you do is select a circle or an arc. That's it. Really.

DIMCONTINUE

Draws a linear, angular, or ordinate dimension that continues from the end of the previous (or a selected) dimension. Unlike DIMBASELINE, the second dimension does not include the first.

 Toolbar: On the Dimension toolbar, click Continue Dimension.

Menu: Choose Dimension⇨Continue.

How to use it

First, select the dimension you want to continue next to. Then point to the second extension line or select the object to dimension.

DIMDIAMETER

Draws a diameter dimension for a circle or an arc.

 Toolbar: On the Dimension toolbar, click Diameter Dimension.

Menu: Choose Dimension⇨Diameter.

How to use it

Select an arc or a circle. Move the cursor and watch the dimension move around. Click when you like what you see.

The Text option enables you to customize the text on the command line. Mtext opens the Multiline Text Editor. In the Text Editor, you see brackets that represent the dimension text AutoCAD thinks you want. You can keep it and add your own text before or after the brackets or delete the brackets and insert your own text.

When you delete the brackets, you lose *associativity*. That means the dimension measurement is not automatically adjusted if you change the size of the object being dimensioned,.

The Angle option changes the angle of the dimension text.

DIMEDIT

Edits dimensions. You can change the dimension text as well as its location. You also have an option for creating *oblique* extension lines, that is, extension lines that come out at some weird angle that happens to suit your needs.

Toolbar: On the Dimension toolbar, click the Dimension Edit button.

Menu: Choose Dimension⇨Oblique — for the Oblique option only of DIMEDIT.

How to use it

This command provides several options:

Home	Moves the dimension text to its default position.
New	Changes dimension text. AutoCAD displays the Multiline Text Editor, enabling you to edit the text.
Rotate	Rotates the text. You tell AutoCAD the angle.
Oblique	Creates oblique extension lines for linear dimensions. Use this command when the regular extension lines interfere with the rest of your drawing. Type the final angle you want for the extension lines (not the change from the current angle).

After you've selected your option, AutoCAD prompts you to select objects (you can select more than one dimension). Select the dimension or dimensions you want to change to complete the command.

More stuff

The DIMTEDIT command moves and rotates dimension text.

DIMLINEAR

Draws linear dimensions.

 Toolbar: On the Dimension toolbar, click the Linear Dimension button.

Menu: Choose Dimension⇨Linear.

How to use it

If you want AutoCAD to automatically create the extension lines, just press Enter and select the object you want to dimension. Otherwise, specify the extension line origins.

Then AutoCAD prompts you for the dimension line location with several options. The Text option enables you to customize the text on the command line. Mtext opens the Multiline Text Editor. In the Text Editor, you see brackets that represent the dimension text AutoCAD thinks you want. You can keep it and add your own text before or after the brackets or delete the brackets and insert your own text.

 When you delete the brackets, you lose *associativity.* That means the dimension measurement is not automatically adjusted if you change the size of the object being dimensioned.

The Angle option changes the angle of the dimension text.

You can also draw Horizontal, Vertical, and Rotated dimension lines.

More stuff

 Remember that the appearance of your dimension is controlled by the DIMSTYLE command. Chapter 10 in *AutoCAD 2000 For Dummies* has more on dimensioning.

DIMORDINATE

Draws ordinate dimensions that mark X or Y coordinates on your model.

 Toolbar: On the Dimension toolbar, click the Ordinate Dimension button.

Menu: Choose Dimension⇨Ordinate.

How to use it

At the prompt, pick the point on your model that you want to dimension. Then pick the endpoint of the leader that leads to the ordinate text. Usually, you can specify either the X or Y point just by placing the text properly — experiment and you'll see how it works. You do, however, have options to force an X or a Y point. You can also choose Text, Mtext, and Angle options to control the text content and angle.

DIMRADIUS

Draws radial dimensions for arcs and circles.

 Toolbar: On the Dimension toolbar, click the Radius Dimension button.

Menu: Choose Dimension⇨Radius.

How to use it

At the prompt, select an arc or a circle. As you move the cursor, the dimension text moves with it. Click when you like what you see.

The Text option enables you to customize the text on the command line. Mtext opens the Multiline Text Editor. In the Text Editor, you see brackets that represent the dimension text AutoCAD thinks you want. You can keep it and add your own text before or after the brackets or delete the brackets and insert your own text.

 When you delete the brackets, you lose *associativity.* That means the dimension measurement is not automatically adjusted if you change the size of the object being dimensioned.

Angle changes the angle of the dimension text.

More stuff

 Remember that the appearance of your dimension is controlled by the DIMSTYLE command. Chapter 10 in *AutoCAD 2000 For Dummies* has more on dimensioning.

DIMSTYLE

Defines dimension settings into dimension styles.

 Toolbar: On the Dimension toolbar, click the Dimension Style button.

Menu: Choose Dimension⇨Style.

How to use it

AutoCAD opens the Dimension Style Manager dialog box, which enables you to control every aspect of the appearance of dimensions. To choose the current dimension style, select a style from the Styles list and click Set Current. To create a new style, click New. Similarly, to modify an existing style, click Modify. You can also override individual settings of existing styles and compare styles.

If you click New, name the new style in the Create New Dimension Style dialog box, and use the Use for drop-down list to choose the type of dimensions to use it for — all dimensions or any one type of dimension, such as linear, angular, or radius. Then click Continue. You are now in the New Dimension Style dialog box, where you define the dimension style.

If you click Modify, you open the Modify Dimension Style dialog box, which is the same as the New Dimension Style dialog box. Here you can make any changes you want to the dimension style.

The New Dimension Style dialog box has the following tabs for defining a dimension style:

+ **Lines and Arrows:** Set the color, lineweight, and spacing of dimension and extension lines. You can also suppress one or both dimension or extension lines. Choose the arrowhead type and color. Decide on the size and type of center mark for circles.

+ **Text:** Set the text style. (See the STYLE command.) Set the text color and height and a scale for fractions (if you are using them). Choose vertical and horizontal text placement — for example, you can center the text within the dimension line for mechanical drawings and place the text above the dimension line for architectural drawings. Click the ellipsis button to open the Text Style dialog box to create a text style.

+ If you set the text style height (using the STYLE command) to 0, the height you set here prevails. If your text style has a height, the text height you set here is ignored.

+ **Fit:** Choose how you want text and arrows to fit within extension lines when you have a short dimension. Decide where text will go when it can't fit. Set the scale factor used for text, arrows, and so on. You can choose to scale the dimensions to the scale used in your paper space layouts. Finally, you can choose to place text manually and always draw a dimension line between extension lines (even if nothing else will fit).

+ **Primary Units:** Decide the type and precision of units for linear and angular dimensions. You can also round-off dimensions and add a prefix or a suffix (such as mm for millimeters) to every dimension. You can change the scale of your actual measurements — for example, use a scale of 25.4 to change your English inch measurements to millimeters. You can suppress zeros either before or after dimensions, for example, change 3'-0" to 3'.

✦ **Alternate Units:** This tab is about the same as the Primary Units tab but you use it to turn on (check Display alternative units) and define alternate units. When you use alternate units, AutoCAD displays your dimensions with two types of units. The most common example is to display both English and metric measurements.

✦ **Tolerances:** A tolerance defines the limits of acceptable precision. Define the tolerance method and precision. Depending on the method, choose an upper and lower value, if applicable. You can also define tolerance height and position and suppress zeros.

Click OK when you are finished defining your dimension style. Whew! Don't forget to save your dimension styles in your templates.

More stuff

See also all the commands starting with *DIM.* See Chapter 10 of *AutoCAD 2000 For Dummies* for the latest and greatest on dimensioning.

DIMTEDIT

Moves and rotates dimension text.

 Toolbar: On the Dimension toolbar, click Dimension Text Edit.

Menu: Choose Dimension⇨Align Text and then choose an option from the submenu.

How to use it

AutoCAD prompts you to select a dimension (first if you use the toolbar, last if you use the menu — go figure!). Then you can pick a point for new text location or select one of the options:

Left	Left-justifies the text along the dimension line
Right	Right-justifies the text along the dimension line
Center	Centers the text along the dimension line
Home	Returns the text to its default location
Angle	Changes the angle of the text

DIST

Measures the distance between two points.

 Toolbar: On the Inquiry flyout of the Standard toolbar, click the Distance button.

Menu: Choose Tools⇨Inquiry⇨Distance.

How to use it

 Pick two points — AutoCAD tells you the distance between them. Use object snaps if possible to ensure accurate measurement.

DIVIDE

Divides an object into even segments, placing a point object or block of your choice at each division point.

Menu: Choose Draw⇨Point⇨Divide.

How to use it

Select an object and tell AutoCAD into how many segments you want to divide it.

More stuff

Use DDPTYPE to control how point objects appear. You may want to choose a more visible point type than you usually use.

You can select the block option and name a block within your drawing. Choose whether or not to align the block with the orientation of your object. AutoCAD divides the object using the block instead of points.

DONUT

Draws donuts (or doughnuts if you're hungry), with or without holes.

Menu: Choose Draw⇨Donut.

How to use it

AutoCAD asks you for inside and outside diameters. If the inside diameter is 0, the donut has no hole. AutoCAD then prompts you for the center of the donut. Press Enter to end the command or you'll be drawing donuts until the police come to eat them up.

More stuff

The fill mode determines whether your donut is filled in (chocolate) or not (vanilla). See the FILL command.

DRAWORDER

Changes the order in which objects are displayed; especially useful for inserted images and solid-filled objects.

 Toolbar: On the Modify II toolbar, click the Draworder button.

Menu: Choose Tools⇨Display Order.

How to use it

You have four options:

Send to back	Sends the selected objects to the back of the draw order so that anything that can hide them will hide them.
Bring to front	Sends the selected objects to the front of the draw order so that they look as if they're on top of everything.
Bring above object	Requires you to choose both the objects you want to move above and one reference object. AutoCAD moves the objects above (in front of) the reference object.
Send under object	Requires you to choose both the objects you want to move under and one reference object. AutoCAD moves the objects under (behind) the reference object.

More stuff

If you use the toolbar, the prompts read somewhat differently, but you'll figure it out. If objects don't have some type of fill, you don't see any difference with DRAWORDER. Use it for imported raster images and objects with a fill or a hatch.

DSETTINGS

 Sets drafting aids such as snap mode, the grid, object snaps, polar tracking, and object snap tracking.

Menu: Choose Tools⇨Drafting Settings.

Shortcut menu: Right-click SNAP, GRID, POLAR, OSNAP, or OTRACK on the status bar and choose Settings.

How to use it

AutoCAD opens the Drafting Settings dialog, which has three tabs.

On the Snap and Grid tab, you can set the snap X and Y spacing. You can change the angle of the snap points and set a new base point for calculating the snap points (other than the default of 0,0). You can also set the grid X and Y spacing. You can also turn snap and grid on.

You can use two kinds of snap. Grid snap creates snap points on a grid, either the usual rectangular grid or an isometric grid if you want to create isometric drawings. (See ISOPLANE for more information.) Polar snap lets you snap to points along an angle, for example, every .5 units along angles in 45-degree increments.

On the Polar Tracking tab, you set the increment angle for polar tracking, such as every 45 degrees. You can add additional angles. You can decide whether you want the calculation of the angles to be absolute or relative to the last segment you drew. Finally, you can decide whether to use the polar tracking angles for object snap tracking or to restrict object snap tracking to 90-degree (orthogonal) angles.

On the Object Snap tab, you choose which object snaps you want.

When you're finished with the dialog box, click OK.

On the status bar, you can click the SNAP, GRIP, POLAR, OSNAP, and OTRACK buttons to turn them off and on.

More stuff

For more information on these drawing aids, see Part I. *See also* the SNAP, GRID, and OSNAP commands. See Chapter 5 of *AutoCAD 2000 For Dummies.*

DSVIEWER

Opens the Aerial View window for quick zooming and panning.

Menu: Choose View⇨Aerial View.

How to use it

AutoCAD opens the Aerial View window with your drawing cozily nestled inside. Although you have a menu, you can do most of the stuff using the buttons. Before you do anything, make sure that the Aerial View window is active — its title bar should be blue, not gray.

Aerial View now works like Zoom Dynamic. Click in the window. When you see a box with an X inside, you can pan. Click once to change to a box with an arrow inside, which lets you zoom. Keep on clicking to keep on switching. When you have the view you want, right-click to create the view in your large window.

The Zoom In button zooms in on the image in the Aerial View window. The Zoom Out button zooms out on the image in the Aerial View window. The Global button enables you to see your entire drawing in the Aerial View window.

DTEXT

Draws text line by line. The *D* stands for *dynamic;* you see the text on-screen as you type it in. (That fact may seem mundane to some of you, but us old fogies remember the days of the plain-Jane TEXT command.)

Menu: Choose Draw⊏▷Text⊏▷Single Line Text.

How to use it

The DTEXT command is suitable for one-line labels.

In AutoCAD 2000, the TEXT and DTEXT commands have been unified. You can use either one. They both act like the DTEXT command in drawings

Pick a start point or provide a justification code or a style. The justification codes offer you many alignment choices for your text. Some of the most useful follow:

Align	Fits your letters between a start point and an endpoint. The size of the letters is adjusted proportionately.
Fit	Fits your letters between a start point and an endpoint, but you specify a height, which remains fixed.
Center	Centers the text around a point on the bottom of the letters.
Middle	Centers text both horizontally and vertically around a point.

Some of the others are TL (Top Left), MC (Middle Center), and BR (Bottom Right). You get the idea.

After you decide on your style and justification, pick a start point. If the current text style has no set height, AutoCAD prompts you for a height. Now start typing. Press Enter to end a line. DTEXT continues to prompt you for new text. Press Enter again after the last line to complete the command.

Note that the text you see on-screen moves to its proper justification only after you complete the command.

More stuff

Use MTEXT for paragraphs. The STYLE command defines text styles. See Chapter 9 of *AutoCAD 2000 For Dummies.*

DVIEW

Creates parallel projection and perspective views in 3D space.

Menu: Choose View↔3D Dynamic View.

How to use it

This is a weird one, but here goes. DVIEW is a way of viewing objects in 3D space, using the concept of a camera and a target. You decide where the camera is and what the target is, and AutoCAD shows you what you would see.

The first prompt is to select objects. Select as few as you can for the sake of speed. At the end of the command, you see all the objects that would be seen by the view you've defined. You can also press Enter, and AutoCAD supplies a picture of a darling, little house. You can use the house model to set the angles and distances and then see your picture after you exit DVIEW.

Type **ca** to place your camera. AutoCAD starts you from the center of the drawing. Try moving the cursor to rotate the imaginary camera. First, you're moving up and down, which technically means changing the angle from the XY plane. It's similar to rolling your eyes up and down. Click the Return (right) button of your mouse when you like what you see. An alternative is to type an angle at the command line. An angle of 0 degrees is looking straight out. An angle of 90 degrees looks down from above. The Toggle Angle option toggles between locking the camera at the specified angle and unlocking it so that you can use the mouse to set it.

Now AutoCAD prompts for the angle relative to the X axis. Again you can use the mouse and right-click to set the angle, or type an angle at the command line. In this case, 0 degrees means you're looking along the X axis toward 0,0. This angle can go from 180 degrees to -180 degrees. (Both mean the same thing, looking along the X axis out towards infinity — sounds enlightening!)

If you just want a parallel projection view and you picked only one object, press Enter to see the view. You're finished.

If several objects are involved, you can set the target. This action creates your line of sight. Type **ta**. The prompts here are the same as for the camera option. You can press Enter and see a parallel projection view.

The Distance option turns on perspective views (where objects that are farther away look smaller). A slider bar appears that you can use to set the distance between the camera and your objects. Drag on the slider bar, move your mouse (watch what happens to the slider bar), or type a number.

The POints option shows you your camera and target points. You can use this option to type new camera and target points (or use object snaps on objects in your drawing).

DVIEW has its own pan and zoom (and so the regular PAN and ZOOM commands can't be used transparently in this command). If you use the Off option to turn off perspective viewing, zoom moves you in to the center of the drawing, using another slider bar. If perspective viewing is on, zooming in has an effect like going from a wide-angle lens to a normal lens to a telephoto lens.

The CLip option creates invisible walls that obscure what's in front of a front-clipping plane and what is behind a back-clipping plane. Pick either Back or Front and use the slider bar to drag the clipping plane. Or you can pick both Back and Front.

The Hide option removes hidden lines (lines that you wouldn't see from the chosen viewing angle) for the selected objects. Wireframe display returns when you exit the DVIEW command.

Keep on using options until you're finished defining the view. (There's an Undo option.) Then press Enter to complete the command and see your view.

More stuff

After you get the view you want, don't expect to ever reproduce it again. So save that view! *See also* VIEW.

DWGPROPS

Sets drawing-wide properties for the current drawing

Menu: Choose File⇨Drawing Properties.

How to use it

Use the Drawing Properties dialog box to set properties that you can use to identify and find your drawing. The General tab contains information you can read but can't change, so move on to the Summary tab, where you can type information for the title, subject, and author. You can also enter keywords and comments that you can use when searching for that lost drawing. The Statistics tells you when your drawing was created and last saved and some other boring stuff.

The Custom tab lets you assign up to 10 custom properties and their values. For example, you could assign each drawing a Coolness Rating.

When you're finished, click OK.

More stuff

You can use some of this information with the Find feature of DesignCenter. Click Find on the DesignCenter toolbar. You can also use the drawing properties in Windows Explorer — right-click on the file name and choose Properties.

EDGE

Sets the visibility of 3D face edges.

 Toolbar: On the Surfaces toolbar, click the Edge button.

Menu: Choose Draw⇨Surfaces⇨Edge.

How to use it

EDGE is used only for objects created with 3DFACE. It makes edges visible and invisible, at your command. Select visible edges to make them invisible. To make invisible edges visible, right-click Display and then use the All default suboption to display invisible edges with dashed lines. Now you can select them to make them visible. Magic! *See also* 3DFACE.

EDGESURF

Draws a 3D polygon mesh surface.

 Toolbar: On the Surfaces toolbar, click the Edge Surface button.

Menu: Choose Draw⇨Surfaces⇨Edge Surface.

How to use it

First, you need four touching lines, arcs, or polylines that together create a closed path. To create the surface, all you do is select a point on each of the four edges, in any order. AutoCAD creates a mesh surface.

More stuff

The surface created by EDGESURF approximates something that mathematicians call a Coons surface patch. Just think of a small corn patch where raccoons come to feed.

ELEV

Sets the elevation (height above the "ground" XY plane) and thickness of new objects.

Command line only

How to use it

AutoCAD prompts you for a new elevation. Type an elevation in units, or press Enter if you want to keep the current distance (which is kindly provided after the prompt). When AutoCAD prompts for a thickness, type a number. A circle with a thickness is a cylinder. Objects with thickness are surfaces, not solids.

All new objects you create are created on the elevation you set until you change the elevation.

More stuff

A negative thickness creates the surface in the direction of the negative Z axis.

ELLIPSE

Draws an ellipse.

 Toolbar: On the Draw toolbar, click the Ellipse button.

Menu: Choose Draw⇨Ellipse.

How to use it

The default is to specify the first endpoint of the first axis. Specify a point. Then specify the other endpoint. AutoCAD asks you for the other axis distance, which is similar to a radius, from the midpoint of the first axis to the edge of the second axis. Specify a point.

You can choose the Center option at the first prompt to draw an ellipse by specifying first its center, then the first axis endpoint, and finally the other axis distance.

Choose the Arc option at the first prompt to draw an elliptical arc. Specify the two endpoints of the first axis and the axis distance. AutoCAD goes on to prompt you for a start angle and an end angle of the arc. You also have an option to specify the included angle, which is the number of degrees included in the arc starting from the start angle.

ERASE

Erases objects.

Toolbar: On the Modify toolbar, click the Erase button.

Menu: Choose Modify⇨Erase.

How to use it

It's simple. Select objects. Press Enter to end the selection process, and AutoCAD makes 'em go away. What's even easier is to forget about the ERASE command altogether. Select the objects first, and then press the DEL key.

More stuff

OOPS restores previously erased objects. U and UNDO undo previous commands and also restore your precious objects.

EXPLODE

Breaks up blocks and other compound objects into individual components.

Toolbar: On the Modify toolbar, click the Explode button.

Menu: Choose Modify⇨Explode.

How to use it

You just select the objects, and AutoCAD explodes them. For example, if you make a block of a square and a circle, you'd have your square and circle back as individual objects.

More stuff

You can explode not only blocks but also polylines, multilines, solids, regions, bodies (sounds messy), and meshes. Also, remember that dimension and hatches are blocks.

See also the BLOCK and XPLODE commands. See Chapter 14 of *AutoCAD 2000 For Dummies* for more.

EXPORT

Translates drawings or objects into other file formats.

Menu: Choose File⇨Export.

How to use it

AutoCAD opens the Export Data dialog box. In the List Files of Type box, choose the format you want to create. In the File Name box, type the name of the file. Click OK. In most cases, AutoCAD prompts you to select objects. AutoCAD then creates the file.

More stuff

AutoCAD has individual commands to export to different formats: ACISOUT, 3DSOUT, WMFOUT, BMPOUT, PSOUT, and STLOUT.

EXTEND

Extends a line, an arc, an open polyline, or a ray to meet another object.

 Toolbar: On the Modify toolbar, click Extend.

Menu: Choose Modify⇨Extend.

How to use it

AutoCAD first prompts you for the boundary edges and asks you to select objects. These are the edges you want to extend *to*. Then you select the object you want extended. AutoCAD repeats this second prompt so that you can extend more objects to the original boundary edge or edges. Press Enter to end the command.

You can quickly select a number of objects to be extended using the Fence object selection method. See the SELECT command.

More stuff

If your objects are 3D, this process gets more complicated because what looks like an intersection of objects in 2D may not be in 3D. Use the Project option. Then project based on the current UCS or the current view, or use the None suboption to project based on true 3D space.

EXTRUDE

Creates simple 3D solids by extruding (pushing out into the third dimension) existing, closed, 2D objects.

 Toolbar: On the Solids toolbar, click the Extrude button.

Menu: Choose Draw⇨Solids⇨Extrude.

How to use it

Select the objects you want to extrude, including closed polylines, circles, polygons, and so on. Don't pick objects that have crossing parts like a figure eight. The default is to then specify a height. (If you enter a negative number, AutoCAD extrudes in the direction of the negative Z axis.) Now AutoCAD asks for an extrusion taper

angle. If you press Enter for the default, which is 0 degrees, you get a solid that rises perpendicular from the original object, with no tapering.

You can specify a taper angle between 0 and 90 degrees to taper in. A taper angle between 0 and -90 degrees tapers out. If the taper angle is too great for the height so that the object would taper to a point before reaching the height you set, AutoCAD refuses to extrude the object.

More stuff

After selecting your objects, you can select the Path option. You select an object to be the path. It can be curved. The path object cannot be in the same plane as the 2D object you're extruding. See Chapter 15 of *AutoCAD 2000 For Dummies* by Bud Smith.

FILL

Sets the fill mode for multilines, solids, solid-filled hatches, and wide polylines.

Command line only

How to use it

You have two choices. On (one) means fillable objects are solidly filled. Off means objects aren't filled. You can also turn FILL on and off on the Display tab of the Options dialog box. See the OPTIONS command.

FILLET

Fillets (rounds off) intersections to make rounded corners.

Toolbar: On the Modify toolbar, click the Fillet button.

Menu: Choose Modify⇔Fillet.

How to use it

The simple way to use this command is to select your first object at the prompt and then select the second object. AutoCAD fillets them. AutoCAD extends or trims your objects as necessary. If one of your objects is an arc or a circle, more than one possible way to fillet may exist. AutoCAD creates a fillet with endpoints closest to the points you used to select the objects.

If you choose the Polyline option and select a polyline, AutoCAD fillets the polyline at every possible vertex.

Choose the Radius option to specify the radius of future fillets. For some reason, this option ends the command, so use it again if you want to fillet something with the new radius.

You have a Trim option. Usually, AutoCAD trims your lines to make a neat fillet, but if you choose No Trim, AutoCAD makes the fillet and leaves the lines, too. A little sloppy, if you ask me.

More stuff

You can also fillet 3D solid objects. If you select a 3D solid object, AutoCAD prompts you accordingly.

FILTER

Creates a filtered list of objects to help you select objects based on their properties.

Command line only

How to use it

You can create a filter first and then use it on an editing command using the Previous option. Generally, you use a filter transparently, within a command. Start the command and, at the Select objects prompt, type **'filter**.

AutoCAD opens the Object Selection Filters dialog box. The top shows your current filter lists, if you have any. Use the Select Filter section to create new filters. Follow these steps:

1. Pick an item from the drop-down list. If the item is an object such as a circle, you can go directly to Step 5. AutoCAD then creates the filter Object = Circle. AutoCAD uses this filter to find objects that are circles.

2. If appropriate, add an operator from the table shown after this list. For example, if you choose Circle Radius, you need to add an operator and a value.

3. If the item has a limited number of values, choose Select and choose the value from the drop-down list. For example, you can choose the name of a layer from the list.

4. If you want to assign a value, type the value next to the X text box. For example, if you choose Circle Radius and the operator is = (equals) you can type 3 to select circles whose radius equals 3.

5. Choose Add to List.

6. Continue to add filter statements to your heart's desire. You can add logical operators (AND, OR, and so on) around them. The logical operators are at the end of the drop-down list of items. Logical operators must be paired before and after the objects they apply to. AND (the default) means that AutoCAD finds objects that meet both criteria. OR means that AutoCAD finds objects that meet either criteria.

7. After you've completed your filtering statements, type a name for your filter next to the Save As box and click Save As. It always pays to save!

8. Click Apply.

9. In your drawing, AutoCAD prompts you to select objects. You thought you just did that! Type **all** or make a window around all the objects you want to apply the filter to. Press Enter to end object selection and presto! Only the objects that satisfy your filter make it through.

10. Now go do something with those objects.

You can use the following operators to define the filter:

Operator	Meaning
=	Equals
!=	Not equal to
>	Greater than
>=	Greater than or equal to
<	Less than
<=	Less than or equal to
*	Equal to any value

More stuff

See also QSELECT, which also creates selection filters, but more easily.

FIND

Finds and replaces text.

Toolbar: On the Standard toolbar, click the Find and Replace button.

Menu: Choose Edit⇨Find.

Shortcut menu: With no command active, right-click in the drawing area and choose Find.

How to use it

AutoCAD opens the Find and Replace dialog box. The FIND command searches the entire drawing by default. If you want to be pickier, click Select objects. AutoCAD returns you to your drawing where you can select objects. Press Enter to return to the dialog box.

Type the word(s) you want to find in the Find text string box. If you just want to find the text, click Find Next. AutoCAD displays the sentence containing the text in the Context area of the dialog box.

If you want to replace the text, type the replacement text in the Replace with box. Then click Find Next and choose Replace or Replace All.

Click Options to limit the find to whole words containing your text or to words exactly matching the case (uppercase or lowercase) of the text you typed.

Click Zoom to if you want to zoom into the area containing the text you typed. Click Close when you're finished.

FOG

Creates a haze effect to simulate distance in 3D rendering — sort of like the air in Los Angeles.

 Toolbar: On the Render toolbar, click Fog.

Menu: Choose View⇨Render⇨Fog.

How to use it

In the Fog/Depth Cue dialog box, click Enable Fog. Then choose a color. White (slide the slider bars to the right) creates a traditional fog effect. Black (slide 'em to the left) creates a typical depth cue effect. You can use any color you want. Click Select Custom Color for maximum choice.

Use Near Distance to set where the fog starts, based on the entire distance from the viewer to the last object in the drawing that you can see. Use Far Distance to set where the fog ends.

Use Near Fog Percentage to set the percentage of fog you want to start with and Far Fog Percentage to set the percentage of fog you want to end up with.

Play around with different settings. Then render the drawing each time to see the results.

GRID

Displays a grid of itsy-bitsy, teeny-weeny black (or white) polka-dots.

Command line only

How to use it

AutoCAD gives you the following options:

Grid spacing(x)	Enables you to type a number to specify the spacing of the grid dots in units. Type a number followed by **x** to set the grid equal to that number times the snap interval.
ON	Turns on the grid.
OFF	Turns off the grid. (Did you guess?)
Snap	Sets the grid spacing equal to the snap interval.
Aspect	Sets the X spacing and Y spacing to different numbers.

Toggle the grid on and off using the GRID button on the status bar.

More stuff

The grid is used to get your bearings. It's useful to set the grid to the snap setting so that you can see where the snap points are. On the other hand, having all those dots on your drawing can be annoying. If you don't like the grid, you don't have to grid and bear it — turn it off. *See also* the SNAP and DSETTINGS commands.

GROUP

Creates a named group of objects that you can select with one pick.

Command line only

How to use it

AutoCAD opens the Object Grouping dialog box. On top is a list of existing groups, if any.

To create a group, type a name in the Group Name text box. You can provide a description of it in the Description text box if you want. In the Create Group section, click Selectable (actually, it's on by default). This option means that when you select one object in the group, you get 'em all, which is the point of creating a group. (But if you need to work with only one object in the group, you might want to turn off the Selectable feature.)

Then click New to create the group. AutoCAD returns you to your drawing. Select the objects for your group and press Enter to complete the selection process. Back at the ranch (the Object Grouping dialog box), y'all click OK to complete the command.

To use the group, just select one object and they all come along.

You can type the group name at the Select objects prompt to select the group.

More stuff

The Change Group section of the Object Grouping dialog box enables you to edit groups. You can remove objects from and add them to the group, change the group's selectable status, or rename it.

HATCHEDIT

Edits a hatch.

Toolbar: On the Modify II toolbar, click the Edit Hatch button.

Menu: Choose Modify➪Hatch.

How to use it

AutoCAD prompts you to select a hatch object. When you do, the Hatchedit dialog box opens, which is the same as the Boundary Hatch dialog box you get with the BHATCH command. Make the changes that you want and click Apply. See the BHATCH command for details on using the dialog box.

HELP

Saves you when you're lost — well, sometimes.

Toolbar: On the Standard toolbar, click the Help button.

Menu: Choose Help➪AutoCAD Help.

How to use it

Use the Contents tab to choose from the various help volumes (the little icons of books). The main volumes are the Command Reference, which lists commands and system variables alphabetically, and the User's Guide, which explains how to accomplish various tasks.

Use the Index tab to type a word and find help relating to that word. Use the Find tab to do a search on a word or a phrase.

You can also get help on a command by starting the command and pressing F1. Choose Help in a dialog box to get help on the dialog box. If the dialog box has a question mark button, click the button and then click on the area of the dialog box that you want help on.

HIDE

Hides lines of a 3D surface or solid object that would naturally be hidden from the 3D view you're using.

 Toolbar: On the Render toolbar, click the Hide button.

Menu: Choose View➪Hide.

How to use it

Before using this command, you need a 3D object. And you need to use VPOINT, DDVPOINT, or 3DORBIT to create a 3D view of your object. Then, when you use HIDE, AutoCAD goes ahead and hides lines that are at the back of your object from your current point of view.

More stuff

HIDE doesn't hide objects on layers that are frozen. *See also* SHADEMODE.

HYPERLINK

 Inserts or edits a hyperlink to an object, enabling you to jump to the other side of the universe from your drawing.

Toolbar: On the Standard toolbar, click the Insert Hyperlink button.

Menu: Choose Insert➪Hyperlink (or press Ctrl+K).

Shortcut menu: To edit a hyperlink, select an object with a hyperlink, right-click in the drawing area, and choose Hyperlink➪Edit Hyperlink.

How to use it

AutoCAD may prompt you to save your drawing if you haven't already. You never know what might happen while you are teleporting through the cosmos. Then select the object.

In the Insert Hyperlink dialog box, type the URL or file name that you want to hyperlink to. You can also click Browse to navigate to a file (and save some typing).

If you want, use the Named location in file box to specify where in the file you want to go. You can use a named view in an AutoCAD drawing, a bookmark in a word processing program, or a named range in a spreadsheet, for example. Why not get exactly where you want to go with one click?

You can create a hyperlink description. AutoCAD uses this description as the tooltip when you pass the cursor over the hyperlink.

More stuff

To edit a hyperlink, select an object with a hyperlink, then right-click and choose Hyperlink⇨Edit Hyperlink. AutoCAD opens the Edit Hyperlink dialog box, which is pretty much the same as the Insert Hyperlink dialog box. One difference is that you can click Remove link to get rid of the hyperlink and stay in the safety of your own drawing.

ID

Gives you the coordinates of a selected point.

 Toolbar: On the Inquiry flyout of the Standard toolbar, click the Locate Point button.

Menu: Choose Tools⇨Inquiry⇨ID Point.

How to use it

 Just pick a point. Using an object snap is a good idea. AutoCAD lists the point's coordinates.

IMAGE & IMAGEATTACH

Attaches *raster* (bitmap) images into your drawings.

 Toolbar: On the Reference toolbar, click the Image button.

Menu: Choose Insert⇨Raster Image.

How to use it

IMAGE opens the Image Manager dialog box, where you can control images in your drawing. From here you can attach, detach, reload, and unload images. Images are generally bitmaps, which means they're made up of little dots (called pixels). Click Attach to attach an image using the Select Image File and Image dialog boxes. (The IMAGEATTACH command opens the Select Image File dialog box immediately for you.) Type the image file name or click Browse to navigate to it and click Open. Check the Specify on-screen boxes to get prompts for the insertion point, scale factor, and rotation angle. Click OK to insert the image.

More stuff

You can insert BMP, TIF, RLE, JPG, GIF, and TGA files. Click Details in the Attach Image dialog box to get resolution and size information about an image.

IMAGEADJUST

Controls the brightness, contrast, and fade of an image.

Toolbar: On the Reference toolbar, click the Image Adjust button.

Menu: Choose Modify⇨Object⇨Image⇨Adjust.

How to use it

Select an image. Use the slider bars to adjust the brightness, contrast, and fade. The preview box enables you to see the result. Click Reset to return to the original settings.

IMAGECLIP

Displays only the portion of an image that's inside a boundary you specify.

Toolbar: On the Reference toolbar, click the Image Clip button.

Menu: Choose Modify⇨Clip⇨Image.

How to use it

At the OFF/ON/Delete/<New Boundary> prompt, right-click to open the shortcut menu and choose Off to turn off an existing boundary, On to turn on an existing boundary that you had turned off, or Delete to delete an existing boundary. To create a new boundary, press Enter or choose New Boundary from the shortcut menu. You then have a choice of creating a polygonal or rectangular boundary. Press Enter to create a rectangular boundary and pick two corners of the rectangle. Right-click and choose Polygonal to create a polygonal boundary and pick all the points you want to create the boundary. Press Enter to complete the boundary. AutoCAD displays only the portion of the image inside the boundary.

IMAGEFRAME

Turns image frames on and off.

 Toolbar: On the Reference toolbar, click the Image Frame button.

Menu: Choose Modify⇨Object⇨Image⇨Frame.

How to use it

By default, images have a frame. You can turn off the frames of all the images in your drawing (right-click and choose Off), for a neater look. Problem is, after turning off the frame, you can't select the images! So turn them back on, of course (right-click and choose On) to edit them.

IMAGEQUALITY

Enables you to display an image at high or draft quality.

 Toolbar: On the Reference toolbar, click the Image Quality button.

Menu: Choose Modify⇨Object⇨Image⇨Quality.

How to use it

This command has two options, High and Draft. Pick one. High quality looks better than Draft quality.

IMPORT

Translates other file formats into AutoCAD drawings.

 Toolbar: On the Insert toolbar, click the Import button.

Menu: Choose Insert⇨3D Studio, ACIS File, Windows Metafile, or Encapsulated PostScript.

How to use it

AutoCAD opens the Import File dialog box. In the List Files of Type list box, select the format type of the file you want to import. Select the filename from the File Name list box.

More stuff

 You also have individual commands for specific formats: the 3DSIN, DXBIN, ACISIN, WMFIN, and PSIN commands. For bitmap files, use IMAGE.

INSERT

Inserts a block or drawing.

 Toolbar: On the Insert flyout of the Draw toolbar, click the Insert Block button.

Menu: Choose Insert⇨Block.

How to use it

AutoCAD opens the Insert dialog box. Type the name of the block or drawing to insert or click Browse. Click Explode if you want the block to be inserted as individual objects.

Check Specify On-Screen if you want to pick the insertion point, scale, and rotation angle on-screen or type your Insertion Point, Scale, and Rotation in the text boxes. Choose OK to insert.

More stuff

If you click Explode and make a mistake, you may have dozens of itty-bitty objects all over your drawing. You can use U to undo the command, but you can also insert the block unexploded first, to see the results and then explode it. You can use the AutoCAD DesignCenter to insert a block from another drawing. See ADCENTER.

 See also the EXPLODE and XPLODE commands for information on exploding blocks. You find out more in Chapter 13 of *AutoCAD 2000 For Dummies.*

INTERFERE

Enables you to create a solid object from the volume where two or more solids intersect.

 Toolbar: On the Solids toolbar, click the Interfere button.

Menu: Choose Draw⇨Solids⇨Interference.

How to use it

AutoCAD prompts you for the first set of solids (after which you press Enter) and then for the second set of solids. Usually, you're just selecting one solid for each set, but you can pick any number. AutoCAD checks the first set against the second set for interference. When you've finished selecting, press Enter and watch AutoCAD figure it out. AutoCAD asks you whether it should create the interference solids. Right-click and choose Yes to create them.

If there is more than one pair of interfering solids, the next prompt begs your permission to highlight pairs of interfering solids. The idea here is that if you've selected lots of solids, the different interfering pairs (I know — we can call them in-laws!) might be hard to distinguish. AutoCAD offers you the opportunity to see the next pair highlighted. Right-click and choose Exit to end the command.

INTERSECT

Creates a region or solid from the overlapping area or volume of two or more regions or solids.

Toolbar: On the Solids Editing toolbar, click the Intersect button.

Menu: Choose Modify⇨Solids Editing⇨Intersect.

How to use it

First, select either regions (2D) or solids (3D). AutoCAD does the rest. What you're left with is only the area or volume that was in common among the selected objects. The rest goes bye-bye.

ISOPLANE

Selects an isometric plane so you can create *isometric* drawings (2D drawings that look like 3D drawings).

Command line only

How to use it

The default at the prompt is a toggle that rotates planes from left to top to right. You can also simply choose Left, Top, or Right. SNAP must be on and set to isometric. You use the DSETTINGS command to turn isometric planes on and off.

LAYER

Everything you always wanted to know about layers.

Toolbar: On the Object Properties toolbar, click the Layers button.

Menu: Choose Format⇨Layer.

How to use it

The Layer Properties Manager dialog box gives you full control over — you guessed it — layers. At the top, the current layer

appears. To create a new layer, click New. AutoCAD names the new layer with a creative name such as Layer1, but highlights it so that you can immediately rename it. Press Enter to lock in the name.

Names can be up to 255 characters long and can include spaces. You can use numbers, letters, and other characters with the exception of the following symbols: < > / \ " : ; ? , * | = '

By default, AutoCAD makes your new layer black/white with a continuous linetype, the default lineweight, and either the Normal plot style or a plot style based on the layer's color. To dress things up a bit, do the following:

✦ Click the color box to open the Select Color dialog box and choose a color.

✦ Click the linetype to open the Select Linetype dialog box and choose a linetype.

✦ Click the lineweight to open the Lineweight dialog box and choose a lineweight.

✦ You can assign a plot style to a layer. For more information, see the PLOT command.

Linetypes have to be loaded the first time you use them. Click Load.

Choose Current if you want your new layer to be the current layer.

You can do four things to layers:

Turn Off and On	On is the normal state for a layer. If you turn it off, the layer becomes invisible, but still regenerates when the drawing regenerates.
Freeze and Thaw	Thawed is the normal state for a layer. If you freeze it, the layer becomes invisible and is not regenerated. You can also freeze and thaw layers in current or new floating viewports, if you're working in a paper space layout.
Lock and Unlock	If you lock a layer, it's visible but can't be edited. This can make it easier to edit overlapping objects on other, unlocked layers.
Plot and No Plot	If you set a layer to No Plot, AutoCAD does not plot anything on that layer.

To change a layer's status, find the column that you want and click the icon. The columns are so tiny that you can't see their heading names. If you hold the mouse cursor over a column, the column's name appears as a tooltip. You can also drag the columns at their heading to change their width.

You can select more than one layer at a time by pressing Ctrl as you click. To select a range of layers, hold down Shift and click the first and last layer you want to choose. Select a layer name again to de-select it. Another trick is to right-click in the Name list area and choose Select All or Clear All from the menu that pops up.

To delete a layer, choose it and click Delete. You can't delete layers that have objects on them.

More stuff

Freezing layers, or turning them off, is useful in a complex drawing. Forgetting what you can't see, however, is all too easy!

Other related commands are COLOR, LINETYPE, PLOT, PSPACE, and VPORTS.

The easiest way to make a layer current is to use the Layer Control drop-down list on the Object Properties toolbar. Just pick the layer you want — but make sure that no object is selected or else you change the object's layer! See Part I for more about layers. Also see Chapters 3 and 5 of *AutoCAD 2000 For Dummies*.

LAYOUT

Creates and manages layout tabs, where you lay out your drawings for plotting.

Toolbar: On the Layouts toolbar, click the New Layout button.

Menu: Choose Insert⇨Layout.

Shortcut menu: Right-click an existing layout tab and choose one of the options.

How to use it

Each layout appears on its own tab. The easiest way to create a new layout is to right-click a layout tab and choose New Layout. You can also copy and rename existing layout tabs the same way.

To switch from one layout to another, click the tab of the layout you want.

More stuff

You can use the AutoCAD DesignCenter to drag a layout from another drawing into your current drawing. *See* ADCENTER.

See also the VPORTS and LAYOUTWIZARD commands for creating floating viewports.

LAYOUTWIZARD

Creates and formats a new layout, including a title block and floating viewports.

Menu: Choose Tools⇨Wizards⇨Create Layout.

How to use it

The Layout wizard creates a layout like the LAYOUT command but goes a lot further. Here's what you can do:

+ Name your layout

+ Choose a printer if necessary

+ Choose a paper size

+ Choose portrait or landscape orientation

+ Choose an existing title block

+ Create viewports and decide how they are configured

Click Finish and voilà! You have a fully formed layout.

More stuff

See the VPORTS and MVIEW commands for more info on creating viewports.

LEADER

See the QLEADER command.

LENGTHEN

Lengthens lines, arcs, open polylines, elliptical arcs, and open splines. Also changes the angle of arcs.

Toolbar: On the Modify toolbar, click the Lengthen button.

Menu: Choose Modify⇨Lengthen.

How to use it

Choose an option. You have four ways to lengthen an object:

Delta	Specifies the increase in length. Or if you select the angle option, specifies the increase in the angle.
Percent	Specifies the increased length as a percentage of its current size. 100 means no change. Type 200 if you want to double the length of the object.
Total	Specifies the total length (or included angle).
Dynamic	Enters Dynamic Dragging mode, enabling you to drag the object to the desired length (or angle).

AutoCAD prompts you to select an object. AutoCAD lengthens a line from the endpoint closest to your selection point. AutoCAD prompts you for more objects to lengthen (as if you have nothing else to do). Press Enter to get on to better things. The Undo option enables you to undo the last lengthen.

LIGHT

Creates lights for use in a rendered scene.

 Toolbar: On the Render toolbar, click the Lights button.

Menu: Choose View⇨Render⇨Light.

How to use it

 This command opens the Lights dialog box. In the Lights list box is a list of all lights you've already defined (if any). Select a light and click the Modify button to modify a light. Modifying a light uses the same dialog box as creating a new one, so refer to the next few paragraphs. Select a light and click the Delete button to delete a light. Click the Select button to return to your drawing so that you can select a light by clicking it — that's if you know where the light is but forgot its name.

On the right side of the dialog box is the Ambient Light section. Ambient light is background, overall light that covers all the surfaces in your drawing. Use the slider bar to adjust the Intensity, or type a number from 0 (no light) to 1 (full brightness). Too low a number can make your drawing appear like a dark room (or a romantic night scene). Too high a number can make your drawing look like an over-exposed photograph. Try starting with 0.3, the default.

In the Color section, choose the ambient light color. You can use the Red, Green, and Blue slider bars, or click Select Custom Color. Maximum red, green, and blue produce white light. (Light colors don't mix like paint colors.)

Now create some lights. (Makes you feel all-powerful, doesn't it?) Next to the New button is a drop-down list of three types of light. Select one of them and click New to create a new light of that type.

Point Light

Choosing Point Light opens the New Point Light dialog box. A point light is like a light bulb. It emits light that radiates out in all directions, and it attenuates, which means the light gets fainter as it gets farther from its source. First, type a name for your light in the Light Name text box (you can use up to eight characters). If you're creating different kinds of lights, it's a good idea to give the lights names that tell you what kind of light it is. For example, you might type PL1 for the first point light. (I'm sure you can be more creative than that, but you get the idea.)

Next, set the Attenuation (how a light fades with distance). You can choose None, Inverse Linear, or Inverse Square. When selecting attenuation, remember that the brightness of inverse square drops off much more quickly than that of inverse linear.

Now set the Intensity of the light, using the slider bar or the text box. The Intensity can be any real number. The default is based on the attenuation setting. Default settings are usually a good place to start.

To set the position of your light, click the Show button to see the current location. AutoCAD automatically places the light at the center of the current viewport. (Point lights radiate light equally in all directions, so there is no target.) You might want to write down the location coordinates. Click OK. Now click Modify. This action returns you to your drawing. AutoCAD has placed a point light block in your drawing so that you can see where it is. You can pick a point or type coordinates. Remember that you usually don't want your light to be "on the ground," so include a Z coordinate.

Finally, select the light's color. This selection works just like the setting for Ambient Light in the Lights dialog box, discussed previously in this section. Check Shadows On if you want to create shadows. Click OK, and you return to the Lights dialog box.

Distant Light

Choose Distant Light from the drop-down box in the Lights dialog box, and click New to get to the New Distant Light dialog box. A distant light produces parallel light beams in one direction and does not attenuate. This light is supposed to be sort of like the sun. (You *are* getting all-powerful here, aren't you?) Type a name for your distant light in the Name text box. The intensity can range from 0 (off) to 1 (full intensity). The color is set in the same way as for Ambient Light in the Lights dialog box, explained previously.

You can set the location of a distant light by using the astronomical terms *azimuth* and *altitude,* or by using the Light Source Vector system. Azimuth means the degrees from north. You can go from -180 to 180, both of which are south. Altitude goes from 0 (ground level) to 90 (straight overhead). In the text box, you can type a number between 0 and -90. You can also use the slider bar. The results of this process are shown in the Light Source Vector section, which defines the light source using X,Y,Z coordinates. Conversely, if you type coordinates in the Light Source Vector section, the Azimuth and Altitude numbers change accordingly.

All these steps are supposed to create a direction for your distant light. If you want, you can create a direction by clicking Modify in the Light Source Vector section. AutoCAD returns you to your drawing and prompts you for a light direction to and a light direction from. You can pick points, but typing them in is more accurate. Remember that the sun usually comes from above the horizon, so you want to pay attention to the Z coordinate. (You don't want to totally change the laws of nature.)

For ultra-realism, click Sun Angle Calculator, which calculates the location of the distant light based on latitude, longitude, and time of day. If you don't know the latitude and longitude, click Geographic Location so you can pick from a list of major cities from around the world or click a location on a map. It's a great way to travel without leaving your chair!

When you're finished, click OK until you return to the Lights dialog box. Click North Location. The default is the positive Y-axis direction but you can change that to any direction you want.

Spotlight

Choose Spotlight from the drop-down list in the Lights dialog box, click New, and you're ready to create a new spotlight. A spotlight produces light in a cone shape, radiating in a specific direction. The New Spotlight dialog box is similar to the New Point Light dialog box, discussed previously in this section. Here are the features that differ:

Position	You need not only a location but also a target.
Hotspot and Falloff	Spotlights have a hotspot, that is, the brightest cone of light. The default is 44 degrees. Falloff is the widest cone of light. The default is 45 degrees. Both can range from 0 to 160 degrees. If the hotspot and falloff angles are the same, the whole cone is bright. If the falloff is a few degrees larger than the hotspot, the result is an area of softer light around the edge of the spotlight. You can get some cool effects this way.

Because spotlights have a location and a target, attenuation is calculated from the location to the object, rather than to the drawing's extents.

More stuff

Use your lights with the SCENE and RENDER commands.

LIMITS

Sets drawing boundaries.

Menu: Choose Format⇨Drawing Limits.

How to use it

To specify the limits with X,Y coordinates, AutoCAD prompts you first for the lower-left corner. These coordinates are usually 0,0. Then type coordinates for the upper-right corner. AutoCAD uses the limits when you use the ZOOM command with the All option and to display the grid.

You can also turn limits checking on. AutoCAD rejects points entered outside the limits. If you feel too rejected, you can turn limits checking off.

LINE

Draws lines.

Toolbar: On the Draw toolbar, click the Line button.

Menu: Choose Draw⇨Line.

How to use it

LINE is surely the most commonly used command in AutoCAD. And it's easy! AutoCAD prompts Specify first point:, and you specify the start of your line. AutoCAD then prompts you to specify the next point, and you specify the endpoint of your line. Often, you want to continue drawing connected lines, so AutoCAD continues to prompt you for points, and you continue to specify endpoints of new line segments until you press Enter to end the command.

At any time, you can right-click and choose Undo to undo your last line segment. Also, if you've drawn more than one line, you can choose Close and AutoCAD closes your lines — that is, draws a line from the endpoint of your last line to the beginning of your first line.

If you end the command and then decide you want to continue drawing lines from the end of the last line (or last arc), press Enter at the `Specify first point:` prompt, and AutoCAD pick ups where you left off.

More stuff

PLINE creates 2D polylines that can have width and can be filled. RAY creates a line that starts but *never* ends. (I just say that to get you interested. But go look it up, and you'll see that I'm right.) XLINE creates a line that never starts or ends but exists nevertheless (it's a riddle). MLINE creates multiple, parallel lines. See Chapter 6 of *AutoCAD 2000 For Dummies*.

LINETYPE

Sets the current linetype, loads new ones, and sets the linetype scale.

Toolbar: On the Object Properties toolbar, click the Linetype Control drop-down list and choose Other.

Menu: Choose Format⇨Linetype.

How to use it

The Linetype Manager dialog box pops open with a list of loaded linetypes. Choose one and click Current to make it current. You can also make a loaded linetype current by choosing it from the Linetype Control drop-down list.

To load a linetype, click Load to go to the Load or Reload Linetypes dialog box. The default file, `acad.lin`, has the standard linetypes, but you can load another file (with the .LIN filename extension) that you've created. Either way, choose a linetype and click OK.

To see the bottom of the dialog box, click Show details. Set the global scale factor to change how noncontinuous linetypes look. If you will plot your drawing at 1:48, set the global scale factor to 48 so the dashes and dots show up on your plot. Set the current object scale to change the scale for just one or two objects whose linetypes don't show up properly — usually because they're too short to display the linetype pattern. Don't forget to change the current object scale back to 1 when you're finished.

More stuff

When you define a layer, you include a linetype. Generally, the best way to use a new linetype is to simply change the layer. Think twice before changing the linetype of objects because this change overrides the layer linetype definition. See the LAYER command for information on creating layers.

LIST

Lists database information for the object or objects you select. This list includes everything that you ever wanted to know about the object and more, including its coordinates, size, layer, and type.

 Toolbar: On the Inquiry flyout of the Standard toolbar, click the List button.

Menu: Choose Tools⇨Inquiry⇨List.

How to use it

I love this command. To find out all about the objects you've drawn is so satisfying. All you do is select objects, and AutoCAD tells all.

More stuff

 You may need to switch to the text screen to see everything AutoCAD has spit out about your object. Press F2. Use F2 again to get back to your drawing.

LOGFILEOFF

Stops recording the text window contents and closes the log file.

Command line only

How to use it

I explain how to use the log file under LOGFILEON. You can also use the OPTIONS command, under the Open and Save tab.

LOGFILEON

Writes to a file the contents of the text window.

Command line only

How to use it

After you turn on the log file, AutoCAD records the contents of the text window each time you enter AutoCAD, until you use LOGFILE-OFF. You can use the log file for troubleshooting.

You can also use the OPTIONS command to turn on the log file. In the Options dialog box, click the Open and Save tab.

More stuff

Each session is separated by a dashed line in the file. This file keeps on growing, so remember to sometimes get rid of the stuff you don't need. Your hard disk will thank you for it. You can change the name and location of the log file using the OPTIONS command (click the Files tab).

LTSCALE

Sets the linetype scale, which is the length of the dashes and spaces relative to the drawing unit.

Command line only

How to use it

AutoCAD prompts you for a new scale factor and gives you the current one for reference. Type a new number. To make the scale smaller — the dashes and dots closer together — type a decimal (or a number smaller than the current scale). Press Enter to end the command. AutoCAD regenerates the drawing with the new scale factor. You can also use the LINETYPE command.

LWEIGHT

Sets the current lineweight, which is the thickness of lines.

Menu: Choose Format⇨Lineweight.

Shortcut menu: Right-click the LWT button on the status bar and choose Settings.

How to use it

AutoCAD opens the Lineweight Settings dialog box. From the Lineweights list, choose a new current lineweight. The Default lineweight is 0.01 inches, or 0.25 mm. You can also set the current lineweight to ByLayer, which means that objects pick up the lineweight assigned to their layer.

You can choose to list lineweights by millimeters (the default) or inches. You can also change the default lineweight. Finally, you can change the display scale for lineweights on the Model tab, if you find it hard to distinguish between different lineweights.

More stuff

When you define a layer, you include a lineweight. Generally, the best way to use a new lineweight is to simply change the layer. Think twice before changing the lineweight of objects because this change overrides the layer lineweight definition. *See* the LAYER command for information on creating layers.

By default, AutoCAD does not display lineweights. Click LWT on the status bar to display them.

MASSPROP

Calculates the mass and other properties of regions or solids.

 Toolbar: On the Inquiry flyout of the Standard toolbar, click the Mass Properties button.

Menu: Choose Tools⇨Inquiry⇨Mass Properties.

How to use it

AutoCAD prompts you to select objects. They need to be regions or 3D solids. Regions are created by the REGION command, more or less for analysis. AutoCAD struts its stuff on the text screen — and it may be a lot — and then asks whether you want to write the information to a file. If you choose Yes, AutoCAD prompts you for a filename.

More stuff

 MASSPROP provides the following information for regions: Area, perimeter, bounding box, centroid (the center of the region), moments of inertia, products of inertia, radii of gyration, and principal moments of inertia. For solids, the command also provides mass and volume. If you have no idea what this stuff is, you probably won't be using this command.

MATCHPROP

Matches the properties of an object or objects to a source object.

 Toolbar: On the Standard toolbar, click the Match Properties button.

Menu: Choose Modify⇨Match Properties.

How to use it

Select the source object whose properties you want to copy. If you want to copy all the properties of the source object, select the destination object(s). Press Enter to end the command. If you're picky, right-click and choose Settings. Here you can choose which properties you want to copy to the destination object(s).

The properties that can be copied are layer, color, linetype, linetype scale, lineweight, thickness, text style, dimension style, and hatch properties. You can't copy a dimension style to an object that isn't a dimension, and so on — you get the idea.

More stuff

You can also select the source object first, then start the command, and finally select the destination object(s). This method is more familiar if you've used the Format Painter in other Windows programs.

MATLIB

Accesses a library of materials that can be imported and exported for use in rendering.

 Toolbar: On the Render toolbar, click the Materials Library button.

Menu: Choose View⇨Render⇨Materials Library.

How to use it

AutoCAD opens the Materials Library dialog box. The Current Drawing list contains materials currently in your drawing. Click Purge to delete all materials that aren't attached to objects. Click Save to open the Library File dialog box and type a name of a different materials library file, including its .MLI extension.

From the Current Library list, choose a material and then click Preview to see how the material looks on a sample sphere or cube. Click Import to add the material to the Materials List. Export moves materials from the Current Materials list to the Current Library list. Click Delete to delete materials from either list. Click Open to open the Library File dialog box, allowing you to open another materials library file. See the RMAT command to attach materials to objects.

MEASURE

Puts points or blocks at specified intervals on an object (sort of like making a ruler).

Menu: Choose Draw⇨Point⇨Measure.

How to use it

AutoCAD prompts you to select the object you want to measure. Select the object, picking a point nearest the end where you want AutoCAD to start measuring. Then specify a distance, called a segment length. MEASURE puts points along the object.

You can instead select the block option, and AutoCAD puts blocks along the object, with the option to align the direction of the blocks with the direction of the object. Use DDPTYPE first to set the point type.

MINSERT

Inserts blocks into a rectangular array in one fell swoop.

Command line only

How to use it

MINSERT prompts you for a block name. Type it or press **?** to get a list. Specify an insertion point. Next, type an X scale factor (the default is 1), a Y scale factor, and a rotation angle. The rotation angle applies to the individual blocks and the entire array. Finally, AutoCAD prompts you for the number of rows and columns and the distance between them.

More stuff

The problem with this command is that after you create the array, the members of the array cannot be changed or exploded.

See also the INSERT and ARRAY commands; MINSERT is essentially a combination of these two commands.

MIRROR

Makes a mirror image of an object.

Toolbar: On the Modify toolbar, click the Mirror button.

Menu: Choose Modify⇨Mirror.

How to use it

Select the object or objects you want to mirror. AutoCAD prompts you to specify points of the mirror line. If you want the line to be at a 90-degree angle, turn on ORTHO to make it easier to specify the mirror line.

AutoCAD asks whether you want to delete the old objects, that is, the objects you selected. If you right-click and choose No (or press Enter), you get both the original and the mirrored version of the object. If you right-click and choose Yes, AutoCAD erases the original objects, and you get just the mirrored version.

More stuff

If the objects you're mirroring contain text, you end up with the text reading right to left. You can tell your client to hold the drawing up to a mirror and read the text through the mirror, but you can also set the MIRRTEXT system variable to 0 to disable mirroring of text when you mirror an object. Type **mirrtext 0** on the command line and press Enter. It's a good thing to know.

MIRROR3D

Draws a mirror image in 3D space.

Menu: Choose Modify⇨3D Operation⇨Mirror 3D.

How to use it

First, select the objects you want to mirror. Then define the plane around which the mirror copy is created. Here are the ways you can define the plane:

3points	The default. Enables you to specify three points on the plane.
Object	Enables you to select a circle, an arc, or a 2D polyline to define the plane.
Last	Uses the last defined plane.
Zaxis	First, pick a point on the plane you're defining. Then pick a point on the Z axis of the plane, that is, a point on a line coming out perpendicular to the plane. (This point is called a point *normal* to the plane.)
View	Pick a point on the viewing plane of the current viewport. AutoCAD uses a plane parallel to the viewing plane that goes through your point.
XY/YZ/ZX	Again, you pick a point on one of the listed planes. AutoCAD uses a plane parallel to that plane but passing through your point.

After you define your plane, AutoCAD asks you whether you want to delete the old objects, just as in the regular MIRROR command. Choose Yes or No (the default) to complete the command.

MLEDIT

Edits the intersections between multiple parallel lines (multilines).

 Toolbar: On the Modify II toolbar, click the Edit Multiline button.

Menu: Choose Modify⇨Object⇨Multiline.

How to use it

Click the image tile that displays the result you want. Some tiles are similar, so you may have to try out a few options before you get what you want. (AutoCAD places a brief explanation of the image tile at the bottom of the dialog box.) Click OK.

AutoCAD prompts you to select the multilines. Sometimes which multiline you select first makes a difference. AutoCAD wisely provides an Undo option so that you can undo the results and try again.

After you're finished, AutoCAD continues to prompt you for more multilines. Press Enter to complete the command.

More stuff

See also MLINE to create multilines and MLSTYLE to manage multiline styles.

MLINE

Draws multiple parallel lines.

Toolbar: On the Draw toolbar, click the Multiline button.

Menu: Choose Draw⇨Multiline.

How to use it

Because multilines are so complicated, they're defined by styles. You usually create a style first and then draw your multiline. When you start MLINE, AutoCAD gives you the current justification, scale, and style and then prompts you for the first point. If you're happy with the settings, just pick a point. When AutoCAD prompts you for the next point, pick one. Continue on, picking points until you're finished. Then press Enter to complete the command. The Close option connects your last multiline segment with the first. Use the Undo option after any segment to delete that segment and try again.

Things really aren't so simple, though. Here are the options:

Justification	Top means that the start point you pick specifies the top line. The other, parallel lines are drawn below. Zero means that the start point you pick is the center of the multiline. The other, parallel lines are drawn equally distant from the start point. Bottom means that your start point specifies the bottom line. The other lines are drawn above. All of this makes sense only if you're drawing a horizontal line from left to right. Otherwise, you need to extrapolate or look at the screen from strange angles — getting a neck ache in the process — to figure out which way is the top and which way is the bottom.
Scale	This scale is a factor of the multiline style definition. That means if you type a scale of 3, and the style says that the lines are to be 1 unit apart, the lines will now be 3 units apart. Type a number.
Style	Type a multiline style or press **?** to get a listing.

After you complete the options, you can start drawing multilines.

More stuff

See MLEDIT to edit multilines and MLSTYLE to manage multiline styles. For the Scale option, you can type negative values to flip the order of the lines. Typing 0 turns the multiline into a single line.

MLSTYLE

Manages styles for multilines.

Menu: Choose Format⇨Multiline Style.

How to use it

This command opens the Multiline Styles dialog box. The top section, called Multiline Style, manages the styles. If the style you want already exists, select it from the Current drop-down list box to make it current. Then click OK and go and make multilines.

Create a new style by following these steps:

1. In the Name text box, type a name. It can be up to 31 characters with no spaces.

2. Click Add to add the style.

3. Click the Element Properties button to open the Element Properties dialog box. Elements are the lines, and they're defined by their offset (distance) from the multiline start point, their color, and their linetype.

4. If you don't want the existing lines, select them and click Delete. You can't delete the last line; you can only edit it.

5. In the Offset text box, type an offset amount. If you want a line right at the start point, your first offset is 0. When creating elements, use positive offset numbers to create lines above the middle of the multiline and negative offset numbers to create lines below.

6. Click Add. The offset appears in the Elements box near the top of the Element Properties dialog box.

7. Click the new element and choose Color. AutoCAD opens the Select Color dialog box, which also appears when you use the COLOR command. (I'm sure that you're reading this book from cover to cover and have already read about COLOR.) Select the color you want or the BYLAYER or BYBLOCK options, and then click OK to return to the Element Properties dialog box.

8. Make sure the element you want to change is highlighted in the Elements box and choose Linetype. AutoCAD opens the Select Linetype dialog box. You can find instructions for it under the LINETYPE command. Select the linetype you want or the BYLAYER or BYBLOCK options, and then click OK. You're back to the Element Properties dialog box again.

9. Repeat Steps 5 through 8 for other lines. Click OK when you're finished with the Element Properties dialog box.

10. Back at the Multiline Styles dialog box, click Multiline Properties to open the Multiline Properties dialog box.

11. Click the Display joints check box if you want to show a short crossline at the vertices of the multiline segments. This display gives an effect somewhat like stained glass.

12. The Caps section controls how the start and end of the multiline are finished off, that is, how you put a cap on the multiline. Choose from Line, which is straight across; Outer arc, which makes a nice semicircle connecting the outer lines; Inner arcs, which makes nice semicircles connecting the inner elements; and Angle, where you can specify lines at an angle.

13. If you want your multiline to be filled in between the lines, go to the Fill section. Choose On to turn background fill on. Click Color to select a color for the background fill. You get the Select Color dialog box again. Choose a color and click OK.

14. Click OK to return to the Multiline Styles dialog box.

15. Under Description, type a suitable description. This description can be pretty long (255 characters) and can include spaces.

16. Click Save. Click Save again in the Save Multiline Style dialog box to save the style in `acad.mln`.

17. Click Load, choose the style from the list, and then click OK. Remember this step or else you won't be able to use your new multiline style later. This process works a bit differently than other loaded, named objects, such as linetypes.

18. Click OK again to complete the command. You're finally finished!

Whew! That's a lot of steps. Are you sure you still want to draw multilines? But after you've created the style, drawing the multilines is fairly simple (see the MLINE command).

MODEL

Switches from a layout tab to the Model tab.

Command line only

How to use it

Actually, you don't use this command at all! If you're on a layout tab, just click the Model tab and be done with it. Same result. The Model tab replaces the TILE button on the status bar in earlier releases of AutoCAD.

MOVE

Moves objects.

 Toolbar: On the Modify toolbar, click the Move button.

Menu: Choose Modify⇨Move.

How to use it

Select your object or objects. AutoCAD prompts for a base point or displacement. Pick a base point. AutoCAD then prompts you for a second point of displacement that shows the distance and location from the base point. You can pick a point, use an object snap, or type a relative coordinate, such as @-2,0. AutoCAD moves your objects as indicated by the distance and direction between the two points.

To use the displacement method, just type the displacement at the first prompt. If you're typing X,Y coordinates, do *not* use @. At the second prompt, press Enter.

More stuff

You can use grips to move objects, too. *See also* GRIPS.

MSPACE

Switches from paper space to model space.

Shortcut: To toggle to MODEL, click PAPER on the status bar or double-click inside a viewport.

How to use it

Because you ordinarily draw in model space, the only reason you'd switch to model space is if you've previously switched to a paper space layout. You switch to paper space to create floating viewports containing different views of your model using the MVIEW command. (I know, floating viewports reminds you of being weightless in a spaceship and floating by a viewport, looking at some asteroid. But sooner or later, you're going to come down to Earth and deal with this stuff.) You have two ways to work in model space:

✦ If you are on the Model tab, you work with no sign of the paper space layout.

✦ If you are on a layout tab, you still see your paper space layout but can work on your model in one of the floating viewports. (You don't generally do serious work on your model in this mode; rather you use it to pan and zoom to get the best view in the viewport.) Use the PAPER/MODEL button on the status bar to switch between paper and model space.

MTEXT

Creates text in paragraph form.

Toolbar: On the Draw toolbar, click the Multiline Text button.

Menu: Choose Draw⇨Text⇨Multiline Text.

How to use it

At the first prompt, specify the first corner of an imaginary boundary for the text. Then AutoCAD prompts you for the opposite corner. The text flows within this boundary. (A bunch of options exist that you can ignore, because you can set them more easily in the Multiline Text Editor.) AutoCAD opens the Multiline Text Editor. Type your text and click OK.

The Multiline Text Editor has three tabs:

Character	Specifies the font, height, and color. You can also choose from bold, italic, and underline styles. Not all fonts support bold and italic. To stack fractions (where one character is on top of another), type the fraction, highlight it, and click the Stack button. To add special symbols, click Symbol and choose from the list. Choose Other from the Symbol list to open Windows Character Map, which contains several fonts of symbols.
Properties	Specifies properties of the paragraph as a whole, such as text style, justification, paragraph width, and rotation.
Find/Replace	Finds the specified text. If you want, you can replace the text with new text.

Click Import Text to open the Import Text File dialog box. Locate any .txt or .rtf (Rich Text Format) file and click Open. The text appears in the text box.

You can create stacked fractions on-the-fly. Type the numerator. Then type a slash (/) to create a horizontal line, a pound symbol (#) to create a diagonal line, or a carat (^) to create a stacked fraction with no line. Finally, type the denominator. When you type a space after the fraction, AutoCAD creates the fraction.

The first time you create an automatic stacked fraction, AutoCAD opens the AutoStack Properties dialog box, where you can customize how automatic stacking works. Make any changes you want and then don't forget to click the Don't show this dialog box option to insert a check mark. Otherwise, you'll get the dialog box every time you create a fraction.

More stuff

Multiline text, also called paragraph text, is one object. In single-line text (created using TEXT or DTEXT), each line is a separate object.

MULTIPLE

Repeats a command until you cancel it.

Command line only

How to use it

After you type **multiple** and press Enter, AutoCAD asks you for a command name. Type it and press Enter. Use the command in the normal fashion. When you're finished, AutoCAD repeats the command, again and again, until you press Esc. MULTIPLE cannot repeat a command that displays a dialog box.

MVIEW

Manages floating viewports. Floating viewports are created in paper space. The viewports themselves are actual objects that you can move, resize, and delete. Their purpose is to set up a final set of views of your objects for printing. They're usually used for 3D objects but can be used for 2D objects as well.

Menu: Choose View⇨Viewports.

How to use it

Before you can use this command, you need to be on a layout tab. The easiest way is to click one of the tabs. This action also automatically puts you into paper space and opens the Page Setup dialog box (by default). See the PAGESETUP command for more information. Click OK or Cancel to get rid of the dialog box. Now, you see your drawing inside two rectangles. The outer, dashed rectangle indicates the printable area of your paper. The inner, continuous rectangle is one floating viewport that AutoCAD created by default. If you're happy with that viewport, you don't need to use MVIEW.

If you want more control over your viewports, delete the viewport just as you would any object. Your drawing disappears! Without a floating viewport, you can't see your drawing on a layout tab.

Now use MVIEW to create new viewports. Choose the number of viewports you want from the submenu. If you choose 2 or 3, AutoCAD gives you further options to specify how the viewports are configured. Or choose New Viewports from the submenu to choose viewport configurations from a dialog box.

Use the Fit option if you want the viewports to fill the entire display. Otherwise, pick two points to specify the outside corners of all the viewports.

Choose Object from the submenu to create a viewport from a closed polyline, ellipse, spline, region, or circle. Choose Polygonal from the submenu to pick points to create a viewport of almost any shape. The prompts are like polyline prompts — you can draw line segments or arcs or both to create weirdly shaped viewports.

When you use MVIEW on the command line, you have more options. The ON and OFF options turn viewports on and off. The Hideplot option lets you hide lines for plotting purposes only in a selected viewport. At the prompt, type **ON** to turn on hidden lines. When AutoCAD prompts you to select an object, select a viewport. To see the result, plot from the layout tab.

You can choose Print Preview from the Standard toolbar to see the result of hiding lines. Another way to hide objects is to open the Properties window (choose Properties on the Standard toolbar) and change the viewport's Hide plot property from No to Yes.

More stuff

If you've saved a viewport configuration using VPORTS, you can restore it using MVIEW. In other words, you can use the same configuration for tiled and floating viewports. Choose View⇨Viewports⇨Named Viewports.

See Chapter 9 in *AutoCAD 2000 for Dummies* for more on layouts and floating viewports.

MVSETUP

Sets up a drawing including specifications for floating viewports. Only for the brave at heart!

Command line only

How to use it

From the Model tab, use MVSETUP to set up a drawing. AutoCAD asks whether you want to enable paper space just in case. If you want to set up a drawing, just say no. MVSETUP walks you through the following prompts:

Units type	Enables you to choose units of measurement (equivalent to using UNITS).
Scale factor	Lists common scale factors. Type a scale factor.
Paper width	Enables you to type a width. This setting is equivalent to the X-coordinate you use with the LIMITS command.
Paper height	Enables you to type a height. This setting is equivalent to the Y-coordinate you use with the LIMITS command.

On the other hand, if you chose Yes to enable paper space, you create floating viewports and lay out your drawing for plotting. Here are your options:

Align	Pans the view in a viewport to align it with a base point of the active viewport. The suboptions are Angled, Horizontal, Vertical alignment, and Rotate view.
Create	Creates and deletes viewports. If you press Enter, you get to create them. The suboptions are Single, Standard Engineering, and Array of viewports. Select the Delete suboption to delete a viewport. Try the Standard Engineering option to get a trial run of what the command does.

Scale	Adjusts the scale factor of the objects in the viewports. The scale factor is the ratio between the paper space size and the scale of the objects. The suboptions enable you to set the scale uniformly for all viewports, or interactively, which means one at a time.
Options	According to the suboption, sets a layer for the title block, resets limits after a title block has been inserted, specifies paper space units, such as inches or millimeters, and chooses whether the title block should be an xref or inserted into the drawing.
Title block	Inserts a title block and sets the drawing origin. When you set the title block, you can choose from a menu of standard sizes. You can choose one and get a default border or choose Add and enter a title block description, filename, and usable area (lower-left and upper-right corners). Selecting the Origin sub-option enables you to relocate the origin point for the drawing.

AutoCAD, in its great wisdom, knows that this is difficult stuff and offers you Undo options at each level.

More stuff

The new LAYOUTWIZARD command is easier to use but it doesn't have the alignment options. *See also* the MSPACE, PSPACE, and MVIEW commands for details about paper space.

NEW

Creates a new drawing.

 Toolbar: On the Standard toolbar, click the New button.

Menu: Choose File⇨New.

How to use it

AutoCAD opens the Create New Drawing dialog box. Here you can choose to use a wizard to set up the new drawing, open a drawing based on a template, or start from scratch using default settings.

More stuff

 Finally, starting a new drawing doesn't close existing open drawings. You can open oodles and oodles of drawings at once if your computer has enough memory to handle it.

OFFSET

Creates new objects at a specified distance from an existing object.

Toolbar: On the Modify toolbar, click the Offset button.

Menu: Choose Modify⇨Offset.

How to use it

First, type the distance of the new object from the existing one. Then AutoCAD prompts you to select an object. When you do so, AutoCAD asks which side. Pick a point on the side of the object where you want the new copy to appear.

You also have an option to pick a point through which the new object passes. This option is a simple way to indicate both the offset distance and the side where the new object appears. Right-click and choose Through, select the object to offset, and pick the Through point.

Either way, AutoCAD continues to prompt you for more offset opportunities. Press Enter to end the command.

OOPS

This cute little command, the only one with a sense of humor, restores erased objects. OOPS restores only the last erased object but does so even after you've used intervening commands.

Command line only

How to use it

After you erase something, just use OOPS to get it back.

More stuff

U and UNDO can also be used to reverse the effect of an ERASE command, if used immediately.

OPEN

Opens an existing drawing.

 Toolbar: On the Standard toolbar, click the Open button.

Menu: Choose File⇨Open.

How to use it

OPEN displays the Select File dialog box, which includes a nice Preview box that shows you what a drawing looks like when you highlight it. Navigate to the drawing's location using the Look in drop-down box. Double-click the drawing's folder in the large box if necessary. When you find the drawing, double-click it or click it once and click Open.

Click Find File to open the Browse/Search dialog box. The Browse tab displays small drawing images. The Search tab enables you to specify a file type, date, or search pattern.

If you know the name of the drawing but aren't sure where it is on the labyrinth that's your hard disk, type the drawing name in the File name box and click Locate. AutoCAD looks, however, in only the search path, which you can set using the OPTIONS command.

You use the OPEN command also to import a drawing interchange file (DXF). A DXF file is a translation of a drawing into a text file, which is an amazing accomplishment. Because many CAD programs accept DXF files, you use DXF to transfer a drawing from one CAD program to another. (Of course, you'd *never* use any CAD program other than AutoCAD, would you?)

First, open a spanking clean, new file using the Start from Scratch option in the Create New Drawing dialog box. Next, choose DXF from the File of Type drop-down list box. Find the DXF file and click Open.

More stuff

You can open a drawing from anywhere on your hard drive, network, or the Internet. For example, you can type the URL of a drawing in the File name text box. You can also click Search the Web to open a browser that lets you browse anywhere on the Web. Click Look in Favorites to open your system's Favorites folder. Click Add to Favorites to add the current folder or a selected file to your Favorites folder.

OPTIONS

Enables you to configure how AutoCAD works (previously the PREFERENCES command).

Menu: Choose Tools⇨Options.

How to use it

This command displays the Options dialog box, which contains the following tabs:

Files	Specifies the all-important search path so that AutoCAD can find hatch file, linetype files, and so on. The Project Files Search Path is where AutoCAD searches for xrefs. The other types of files are fairly self-explanatory. Use the Browse command to navigate to the paths and files you need. Click Add to add a new folder to a search path; don't delete any default entries because without them, AutoCAD might have trouble finding the files you need.
Display	Turns on the old screen menu, turns off the scroll bars if you never use them (most people don't), changes the size of the command line area, and changes the colors and fonts of the screen. You can configure how layouts look. Use the Display Resolution section to fine-tune how objects in your drawing are displayed. You can also improve performance by turning off certain types of display elements.
Open and Save	Sets how often AutoCAD automatically saves your drawing — very important! You can also turn the log file on or off, turn off the creation of backup (*.bak) files whenever you save a drawing, and turn off the preview image you see when you open a file. You can choose to automatically save your drawings in a prior-release format. Finally, you can customize the demand loading of xrefs and ObjectARX applications.
Plotting	Sets your default plotter. Click Add or Configure Plotters to add or configure a plotter. You decide here which type of plot style you want to use for future new drawings (and earlier release drawings that you save in AutoCAD 2000). Click Add or Edit Plot Style Tables to . . . yes, you guessed it. For more information, see the STYLESMANAGER command.
System	Turns off the multiple-drawing interface, gets rid of the startup dialog that appears whenever you open AutoCAD, and changes the pointing device. Click Properties to configure your graphics display.
User Preferences	Customizes what happens when you right-click (and get rid of those shortcut menus if you hate them). You can also set default units for drawings and blocks inserted from the AutoCAD Design Center. You also have settings for hyperlinks, object sorting, and lineweight defaults. You can return to the AutoCAD classic (sounds like a soft drink) keyboard shortcuts — such as Ctrl+C for cancel instead of Copy to Clipboard.
Drafting	Customizes AutoSnap and AutoTrack settings on this tab.
Selection	Controls the pickbox and grip size. You can also customize how grips work. Finally, you can control how objects are selected, including:

	Noun/Verb Selection	On by default. Enables you to select objects before starting a command. You can then give a command that applies to the selected objects. Even with this option on, you can still do it the old-fashioned AutoCAD way — command first.

Use Shift to Add	Requires you to hold down the Shift key to add more objects, as per the Windows custom.
Press and Drag	Requires you to hold down the pick button of your mouse and drag when creating a selection window.
Implied Windowing	On by default. When you click on an empty spot on your screen, AutoCAD assumes that you want to create a window. If you turn it off, you have to type the w (windows) or c (crossing) option to create a window to select objects. (See the SELECT command.)
Object Grouping	Enables you to place objects in named groups.
Associative Hatch	Selecting an associative hatch also selects its boundary.

Profiles	Manages profiles, which are collections of settings that you define using the OPTIONS command. This way, you can quickly change a whole bunch of settings to work in a different way. (Or maybe you share your computer, and you and your computer mate like to work differently.) You can change the current profile or create a new one by clicking Copy and then making changes using the other tabs of the Preferences dialog box. Then click Export to save the profile as an ARG file. After you have your profiles, choose one and click Set Current to use it.

ORTHO

Restricts the cursor to horizontal and vertical directions. Very helpful in creating nice straight lines.

On the status bar, click Ortho.

How to use it

You just click to turn it on or off. If you're using a user coordinate system or snap rotation, ORTHO is set horizontally and vertically to those settings.

OSNAP

Sets object snap modes that continue in effect until you turn them off. These are called running object snap modes. Object snaps are called Osnaps for short.

Toolbar: On the Object Snap flyout of the Standard toolbar, click the Object Snap Settings button.

Menu: Choose Tools⇨Drafting Settings.

Shortcut menu: On the status bar, right-click the OSNAP button and choose Settings.

How to use it

AutoCAD opens the Drafting Settings dialog box with the Object Snap tab on top. Click the object snaps you want. You can also click Clear All to turn off all the object snaps or Select All to turn them all on.

More stuff

 See Chapter 3 of *AutoCAD 2000 For Dummies.* Note that if you turn on the OSNAP button on the status bar and no running object snaps are set, AutoCAD opens the Drafting Settings dialog box for you, as if to say, "And which osnaps would you like today?"

PAGESETUP

 Sets up a paper space layout, including the plotter, paper size, plot area, paper orientation, and scale for each new layout.

Menu: Choose File⇨Page Setup.

Shortcut menu: Right-click the Model tab or a layout tab, and then choose Page Setup.

How to use it

PAGESETUP opens the Page Setup dialog box, which opens automatically (by default) when you display a layout tab for the first time.

At the top left is the current layout name. You can change the name by typing a new name.

You can also change a layout name by right-clicking a layout tab and choosing Rename.

At the top right is a drop-down list of page setup names. You don't need to name your page setups but if you like the settings, you should name and save them. Click Add to save a new page setup. The new page setup is then available whenever you want to use it on other layout tabs.

The Layout Settings tab

The Layout Settings tab lets you choose a paper size from those available for your plotter. You can also change the orientation of the paper. You see a little picture of a piece of paper that shows how your paper is placed in your plotter. The small uppercase *A* on the paper shows how your drawing is oriented in relation to the paper. Sometimes, you have to look at this picture sideways (getting a neck ache as a result) to figure it out.

You can also check Plot upside-down. The combination of setting the orientation and choosing whether or not to plot upside-down is the AutoCAD 2000 method for rotating your plot on the paper.

You can choose what area to plot and the plot scale. There's an easy drop-down list of plot scales that you can use if you're using a standard plot scale. Remember, though, that if you are going to plot from a layout, you usually set the zoom scale in each viewport and then plot at 1:1. Use the Plot Offset section to move the plot away from the lower-left corner of the plot area.

In the Plot Options section, you can turn lineweights on and off (if Plot with Styles is not checked), choose whether or not to use plot styles, plot model space objects before paper space objects, and hide objects. The option to hide objects applies to objects in *only* paper space. For the more typical situation where you want to hide 3D objects in model space, use the Hideplot option of the MVIEW command.

The Plot Device tab

Use the Plot Device tab to choose a plotter or a printer for the current layout. You can click Properties to change the properties of the selected plotter. From the Plot Style Table section, you can choose from a list of plot styles — the type of plot styles available depend on type of plot styles chosen on the Plotting tab. Click Edit to open a selected plot style table. Click New to create a new plot style table. To use a plot style table, you need to check the Display plot styles check box. *See also* STYLESMANAGER for more information on plot styles.

If you think you're ready to plot, click Plot. Usually, you want to fiddle around with your layout first, so just click OK.

PAN

Moves the drawing display so that you get to see something new and different.

 Toolbar: On the Standard toolbar, click the Pan button.

Menu: Choose View⇨Pan⇨Real Time.

How to use it

Just press the mouse button and drag in the direction you want to pan. You must press Esc or Enter, or start a command, to exit this mode. Right-clicking opens up a shortcut menu, where you can change to real-time zoom or choose Exit to exit real-time zoom and pan mode.

More stuff

You can also use the scroll bars to pan vertically and horizontally. As mentioned in Part I, if you have an IntelliMouse, you can press and roll the wheel to pan.

PARTIALOAD

Loads additional objects into a drawing that you have partially opened.

Menu: Choose File⇨Partial Load.

How to use it

You can use PARTIALOAD only if you have used PARTIALOPEN to open the drawing. In the Partial Load dialog box, choose the layers you want to load to add to those that you have previously loaded using PARTIALOPEN. You can also choose a named view from the list or pick a window, but AutoCAD still loads only the layers you choose from within that view or window. *See also* the PARTIALOPEN command.

PARTIALOPEN

Opens part of a drawing, based on a list of layers and named views.

Menu: Choose File⇨Open, and then click Partial Open in the Open dialog box.

How to use it

In the Partial Open dialog box, choose the layers you want to load. AutoCAD loads only the layers you choose. You must choose at least one layer with objects on it to end up with anything in your drawing. You can also choose any existing named view — if you do so, AutoCAD loads objects on the layers you chose within the limits

of the named view. Then click Open to open the drawing as you specified. *See also* the PARTIALOAD command. PARTIALOPEN works with only AutoCAD 2000 drawings.

PASTEBLOCK

Pastes objects that you have copied to the Windows clipboard as a block in a new drawing.

Menu: Choose Edit⇨Paste as Block.

Shortcut menu: With no active command, right-click in the drawing area and choose Paste as Block.

How to use it

First, copy some objects to the clipboard. Then go to an existing drawing or start a new drawing. Now, when you start the PASTEBLOCK command, AutoCAD prompts you to specify an insertion point. The objects are inserted as one block.

More stuff

AutoCAD makes up a weird name for the block, such as A$C76D53A5E. *See also* the BLOCK and INSERT commands for more information on blocks.

PASTECLIP

Inserts data from the Windows clipboard into your drawing.

Toolbar: On the Standard toolbar, click the Paste button.

Menu: Choose Edit⇨Paste.

Shortcut menu: With no command active, right-click in the drawing area and choose Paste.

Keyboard shortcut: Ctrl+V (in the drawing area).

How to use it

If you've used other Windows programs, you probably know that you need to get data — which can be drawing objects, raster images, text, and other data — onto the clipboard first. You do this using the CUTCLIP or COPYCLIP commands.

Then, when you start PASTECLIP, if the data contains drawing objects, AutoCAD asks you for an insertion point. Plain text is inserted at the top-left corner of the current display as multiline text. (You can then edit and format it.) Other types of data, such as objects created in other applications, are inserted as embedded objects, which you can double-click and edit using their original application.

For certain objects, AutoCAD opens the OLE Properties dialog box so you can fine-tune the size and scale of the object. You can also specify text size and plotting quality.

PASTEORIG

Pastes an object into a drawing using the coordinates from the original drawing.

Menu: Choose Edit⇨Paste to Original Coordinates.

Shortcut menu: With no command active, right-click in the drawing area and choose Paste to Original Coordinates.

How to use it

First, copy an object or objects from one drawing to the clipboard. Then move to another drawing. You want the objects to be inserted at the exact coordinates as in the first drawing. Start the command and — poof! — your objects are in your drawing in the exact right spot.

PASTESPEC

Controls how data is pasted into your drawing from the Windows clipboard.

Menu: Choose Edit⇨Paste Special.

How to use it

First you need to get some data onto the clipboard, using CUTCLIP or COPYCLIP. When you start PASTESPEC, AutoCAD opens the Paste Special dialog box. Choose one of the formats from the list. AutoCAD Entities, one of the options you usually see, is the same as AutoCAD objects.

Then choose Paste to simply paste the data into your drawing. Choose Paste Link to create a link to the file that the data came from. That way, if the data is changed in the source file, AutoCAD automatically updates the data in your drawing. Paste Link is for people who always like their data to be up to date. Then click OK.

If you chose to insert the data as AutoCAD objects or an image, AutoCAD asks you for an insertion point. Otherwise, AutoCAD generally places the data at the top-left corner of your current display.

For certain objects, AutoCAD opens the OLE Properties dialog box so you can fine-tune the size and scale of the object. You can also specify text size and plotting quality.

PEDIT

Edits polylines and 3D polygon meshes.

Toolbar: On the Modify II toolbar, click the Edit Polyline button.

Menu: Choose Modify⇨Polyline.

Shortcut menu: Select a polyline, right-click in the drawing area, and choose Polyline Edit.

How to use it

Select a 2D polyline. AutoCAD offers the following options:

Close/Open		If the polyline is closed, enables you to choose Open to remove the closing segment. If it's open, choose Close to close it.
Join		If other objects are connected to the polyline, enables you to join them into the Polyline Club with this option. Choose Join and select the attached objects. The objects never decline to join, unlike some people.
Width		Specifies a width for the entire polyline.
Edit vertex		Offers you the following list of submenu options. PEDIT puts an X at the first vertex so that you know which vertex you're editing.
	Next	Moves the X to the next vertex. It stops at the last vertex.
	Previous	Moves the X marker to the previous vertex. If you've used Next to get to the last vertex, this is how you get back to the beginning.
	Break	Breaks the polyline into two pieces. However, this offers you a sub-submenu. (Are you following me here?) If you just type **go**, AutoCAD breaks the polyline. However, AutoCAD holds the current vertex, and if you use Next or Previous to specify the other end of the break and then use **go**, AutoCAD breaks the polyline between the two vertices, leaving a hole.
	Insert	Adds a new vertex after the vertex marked with the X. You pick a point for the location of the new vertex.
	Move	Moves the vertex with the X. You specify the new location.
	Regen	Regenerates the polyline.

(continued)

	Straighten	Offers the same sub-submenu as Break and works the same way. Replaces the vertice with a straight line.
	Tangent	Marks a tangent direction to the vertex with the X, which can be used for curve fitting, that is, the Fit and Spline options. You specify a point or angle to indicate the direction of the tangent.
	Width	Edits the start and end widths for the segment after the marked vertex. Type a starting and ending width. Use the Regen option to see the results.
	eXit	Exits the Edit vertex submenu and returns you to the original PEDIT prompt.
Fit		Turns the polyline into a smooth curve.
Spline		A spline is a mathematically constructed curve that uses the vertices of your polyline as the frame of the curve. You can control which type of spline you create using system variables. At any rate, just choose this option, and AutoCAD makes your spline.
Decurve		Undoes the results of the Fit and Spline options.
Ltype gen		ON generates a linetype continuously through the vertices of the polyline. OFF starts each vertex with a dash. This option is meaningless if you're using a continuous linetype.
Undo		Undoes operations one by one back to the beginning of your PEDIT session (which may seem like ages ago).

More stuff

If you select a 3D polyline curve (created with the 3DPOLY command), the prompts are slightly different, but not much. If you select a 3D polygon mesh, you also get similar prompts, but with more Edit vertex options because you can move the vertex in three dimensions, using the M and N dimensions.

 How do you turn ordinary lines and arcs into a polyline? Use this command and select attached lines and arcs. AutoCAD informs you that this is not a polyline and asks whether you want to turn it into one. Type **y** and there you go!

PLAN

Shows the plan view of a user coordinate system (UCS).

Menu: Choose View⇨3D Viewpoint⇨Plan View.

How to use it

The plan view is the one looking down from the top — the regular, old 2D way of looking at things. Use the Current option or press Enter to get the plan view of the current UCS.

Use the UCS option to switch to a plan view of a named UCS you've saved. Type the name. If you forget it, right-click and choose the **?** option. Then press Enter and AutoCAD lists named UCSs for you. *See also* the UCS command for more information.

The World option returns you to the plan view of the world coordinate system.

PLINE

Draws a 2D polyline, which is a connected series of lines and arcs that is one object.

Toolbar: On the Draw toolbar, click the Polyline button.

Menu: Choose Draw⇨Polyline.

How to use it

AutoCAD prompts you for your start point. Specify a point. The next prompt offers the following options:

Endpoint of line	The default. When you pick a point, you get a line.
Arc	Right-click and choose Arc to switch into Arc mode. This option has its own submenu:

	Endpoint of arc	The default. Pick a point.
	Angle	Type an included angle for the arc. A positive angle draws the arc counterclockwise. A negative angle goes clockwise. Then you get the rest of the standard options for drawing an arc. (See also the ARC command.)
	Center	Specify a point for the center of the arc. Again, you then get the rest of the standard arc options.
	Close	Close your polyline with an arc.
	Direction	Pick a point to indicate a direction from the start point of the arc. Then pick an endpoint.
	Halfwidth	The halfwidth is the distance from the center of the polyline to its edge. Usually, you type a distance. You can pick different starting and ending halfwidths for a tapered arc segment. I'm not sure how useful this is for drafting, but the results look pretty.

(continued)

	Line	Returns PEDIT to line mode.
	Radius	Pick a point for the radius of the arc. AutoCAD continues to give you standard arc prompts so that you can finish the arc. (Don't delay finishing the arc, because it's going to start raining any day now.)
	Second pt	Complete the arc by specifying second points and endpoints.
	Undo	Undo the last arc segment you created. You *never* need this option!
	Width	Like halfwidth, but you specify the whole width instead of the halfwidth.
Close		Draws a line from the end to the start of the polyline, closing it.
Halfwidth		See the Arc submenu options.
Length		Picking a point specifies the length of the next line segment, which is drawn in the same direction as the previous one.
Undo		See the Arc submenu options.
Width		See the Arc submenu options.

More stuff

The PEDIT command edits polylines. For much more on polylines, see Chapter 6 of *AutoCAD 2000 For Dummies.*

PLOT

Plots or prints a drawing.

Toolbar: On the Standard toolbar, click the Plot button.

Menu: Choose File➪Plot.

How to use it

AutoCAD opens the Fast Track to Plotting Help, which *strongly* urges you to review the special help related to plotting. You should certainly do so, at least the first time you plot using AutoCAD 2000. Although AutoCAD 2000 has improved many plotting features, they're so different from before that you should expect to be confused for a while!

Assuming you've read the plotting help and returned, AutoCAD opens the Plot dialog box. It's a big one, with two tabs, but here goes.

Try a full preview (explained later in this section) first. If everything looks hunky-dory, click OK to plot. (You're very lucky!)

The Plot Settings tab

You may have noticed that this dialog box is similar to the Layout Settings tab of the Page Setup dialog box that appears whenever you first display a layout tab.

Use the Paper Size and Paper Units section to choose a paper size from the drop-down list and choose the units to use (inches or millimeters). You see both the full paper size as well as the printable area.

Use the Drawing Orientation area to rotate your plot on the paper. Watch the picture of the paper and the letter "A" as you choose landscape or portrait. You can also check or uncheck the Plot Upside Down option.

Use the Plot Area section to decide what you want to print — the entire layout (if you're currently on a layout tab), the drawing limits, the drawing extents, the current display, or a named view, if you've saved one. You can also click Window and define the area you want to plot.

Use the Plot Scale section to set your scale factor. If you are on a layout, the default is 1=1. If you are on the Model tab, the default is Scale to Fit. You can choose from the drop-down list or type your own scale. The format is plotted units = real-life units. Real-life units are the same as drawing units because you draw full size. Therefore, a scale of 1=48 using inches as the units means that 1 inch on the final plot is equal to 48 inches in real life. You have shrunk the house to 1/48 of its real size to fit it on the paper.

The Plot Offset section moves the drawing from the lower-left corner of the drawing area, if you so choose. You can also center the drawing.

In the Plot Options sections are some miscellaneous settings that couldn't find any other home. You can choose to plot with or without lineweights and plot styles, you can plot model space or paper space objects last, and you can hide hidden lines for 3D paper space objects.

When you're finished, check it all out by clicking Full Preview. Unless you have a huge drawing, don't use Partial Preview because it isn't very helpful.

The Plot Device tab

In the Plotter Configuration section, you can choose a plotter or printer. Click Properties to fine-tune the plotter settings.

In the Plot Style Table section, you can choose a plot style table. For more information, see the STYLESMANAGER command. You can use plot styles to control how objects plot and to assign pens on a pen plotter.

In the What to Plot section, you can plot the current tab or all the tabs. You can also finally plot more than one copy of a drawing with one command.

Check Plot to File to create a plot file instead of a paper plot. Set the name and location. You can click the Browse the Web button or the ellipse button to browse to the desired location.

When you're finished, you can preview your plot. Choose Partial to see just a rectangle representing your precious drawing in a bigger rectangle representing the paper. Choose Full to get an accurate image of your drawing, including a shortcut menu that lets you pan and zoom. Press Enter or Esc to return to the Plot dialog box.

Turn on your plotter. Load paper in the plotter. Click OK and the plot starts.

Creating drawings for the Web

In Release 14, you created drawings for display on the Internet in DWF (Drawing Web File) format using the DWFOUT format. Now you use the PLOT command. AutoCAD calls this type of plot an *ePlot.*

First, set up the view of the drawing the way you want it to appear on the Web. Saved views are also available so that you can save several views. AutoCAD automatically assigns the file the same name as your drawing, but with the .dwf extension, but you can change that.

Now start the PLOT command and make any other adjustments you want to the PLOT dialog box. On the Plot Device tab, click the drop-down list in the Plotter Configuration section. Lo and behold, you have something called DWF ePlot.pc3. Choose this strange sounding plotter. Notice that you are now plotting to a file, so you can change the name and location. Click OK. AutoCAD creates the DWF file but leaves the Plot dialog box open. If you don't need it, click Cancel.

To view the DWF file on the Web, you have to save it to a Web site using the procedures required by your Internet service provider. Next, you need the WHIP! plugin, which comes with AutoCAD. Then, when you use your browser to view a page that contains a DWF file, WHIP! automatically kicks in. Right-click the drawing to open the WHIP! menu, whose options enable you to pan, zoom, and print.

Want to see how WHIP! works but don't have a Web site to upload your DWF drawing to? Your browser can browse DWF drawings on your very own hard drive. It's kind of like surfing in your living room, but hey! it works. Open your browser, but don't connect to the Internet. In the URL text box, type the path to your DWF file. Voilà!

See Chapter 9 of *AutoCAD 2000 For Dummies* for a full chapter's worth of plotting.

PLOTSTYLE

Sets the current plot style for new objects, or changes the plot style of selected objects.

Command line only

How to use it

For more information on plot styles and plot style tables, including how to create your own, see the STYLESMANAGER command.

PLOTSTYLE applies only if you are in named plot style mode. You can then set a current plot style for new objects or change the plot style of selected objects, in much the same way that you can set a current linetype or change the linetype of an existing object. (In color-dependent plot style mode, plot styles are attached according to the color of the object.) Just as you usually assign a linetype to an object by creating a layer with that linetype, you usually assign a plot style to an object by creating a layer with that plot style. So what I'm saying is that you shouldn't use this command very often.

But if you must, here's how. AutoCAD opens the Current Plot Style dialog box if you have not selected any objects; if you have, AutoCAD opens the Select Plot Style dialog box. Not to worry, they are more or less the same.

At the bottom of the dialog box, choose the plot style table you want to make active from the drop-down list. Then choose the plot style you want from the Plot Styles list. If you want to edit a plot style table, click Editor. When you're finished, click OK.

More stuff

You can see the results of plot styles on a layout tab. Click a layout tab. When the Page Setup dialog box appears (if it doesn't, right-click the layout's tab and choose Page Setup), click the Plot Device tab. Check Display Plot Styles. Another way is to choose Print Preview on the Standard toolbar.

PLOTTERMANAGER

Displays the Plotters folder, where you can start the Add-a-Plotter wizard or use the Plotter Configuration Editor to edit an existing plot configuration (PC3) file.

Menu: Choose File⇨Plotter Manager.

How to use it

The Acad2000\Plotters folder contains plot configuration files that store settings for plotters. You can also use Add-a-Plotter wizard for creating new plot configuration files.

To create a new plot configuration file, double-click the Add-a-Plotter wizard icon. The wizard guides you through the process of choosing whether the plotter is networked or not, naming the plotter manufacturer and model, importing settings from existing plot configuration files (from earlier releases of AutoCAD), deciding whether you want to plot to a port, a file, or AutoSpool, and giving your plotter a cute name. (You get to decide whether your plotter is male or female.)

To edit an existing PC3 file, double-click one of the plot configuration file icons. AutoCAD opens the Plotter Configuration Editor, which is really a dialog box with three tabs:

✦ The General tab displays some information. You can add a description for the configuration file.

✦ The Ports tab enables you to choose a port, plot to a file, or plot to AutoSpool.

✦ The Device and Document Setting tab is where most of the action is. You see a tree structure listing the properties of the plotter. Click any plus sign to open up a listing for a property. To change a property, select it. The bottom half of the dialog box magically adjusts to reveal the options for that property. Properties you can change are media (paper source, size, and so on), pen configurations for pen plotters, graphics settings, calibration, and custom paper sizes.

Make the changes you want and click OK.

POINT

Draws a point.

 Toolbar: On the Draw toolbar, click the Point button.

Menu: Choose Draw⇨Point⇨Single Point, or Draw⇨Point⇨Multiple Point.

How to use it

AutoCAD prompts you to specify a point (meaning a coordinate) and then draws a point (meaning a point object).

More stuff

Unless you chose Single Point from the menu, you have to press Esc to end the command. Use DDPTYPE to determine how points appear.

POLYGON

Draws a polygon using polylines.

Toolbar: On the Draw toolbar, click the Polygon button.

Menu: Choose Draw⇨Polygon.

How to use it

POLYGON asks you for the number of sides. You can type any number from 3 to 1,024. Next, you specify the center. Now comes the interesting part. Your choices are:

Inscribed in circle	Enables you to specify a circle radius. The vertices of the polygon will be on the circle (so that the polygon will be inside the circle).
Circumscribed about circle	Enables you to specify a circle radius. The mid-points of each side of the polygon will lie on the circle (so that the polygon will be outside the circle).

The circle doesn't really exist; it's just a way of defining the polygon.

Instead of specifying the center, you can right-click and choose Edge, and then specify two points that define the endpoints of the first edge. (You can specify the second point using relative coordinates.)

Because the polygon is a polyline, you can use PEDIT to edit it.

PROPERTIES

Modifies the properties of objects.

Toolbar: On the Standard toolbar, click the Properties button.

Menu: Choose Tools⇨Properties.

Shortcut menu: Select an object or objects, right-click in the drawing area, and choose Properties.

Keyboard shortcut: Ctrl+1 (both opens and closes the Properties window).

How to use it

AutoCAD opens the Properties window (also known as the Object Properties Manager), shown in the figure. The Properties window is AutoCAD 2000's new and cool way to change the properties of objects. If you want, you can dock the Properties window (mine seems to like the right side of my screen) and keep it open as you work. You can resize it by placing the cursor over a side and dragging when you see the double-headed arrow cursor.

Properties - My Wonderful Drawing.dwg	
No selection	
Alphabetic	Categorized
General	
Color	■ ByLayer
Layer	0
Linetype	—— ByLayer
Linetype scale	1.0000
Lineweight	—— ByLayer
Thickness	0.0000
Plot style	
Plot style	ByLayer
Plot style table	None
Plot table attached to	Model
Plot table type	Not available
View	
Center X	8.7494
Center Y	4.5393
Center Z	0.0000
Height	9.0838
Width	17.5084
Misc	
UCS icon On	Yes
UCS icon at origin	Yes
UCS per viewport	Yes
UCS Name	

The Properties window automatically changes based on which objects are selected, if any. If you select different types of objects, such as lines and circles, you can change any properties that they have in common, such as layer, color, and so on. If you have several objects selected, but decide you want to work on the properties of only one type of object, you can use the drop-down list at the top of the window to select the objects you want to work with. You can also click Quick Select to filter a selection of objects. (For more information, see the QSELECT command.)

The Alphabetic and Categorized tabs show the same information — it's just organized differently. Try each tab and decide which you like best. You'll probably stick with that tab for the long haul.

To change a property, click its name. For example, to change the layer, click Layer. If the property has a number of possible settings, a drop-down arrow appears in the right column so you can choose the setting you want. So if you have more than one layer in your drawing, you can click the drop-down arrow and choose a layer. If no objects are selected, changing the layer means changing the current layer for future objects that you draw. If objects are selected, changing the layer means you are changing the layer of those selected objects.

For other properties, you type a value. For example, to change the current thickness or the thickness of a selected object or objects, click Thickness. Then type a new value in the right column and press Enter.

For coordinates, the Properties window displays a Pick Point button. Click it to pick a point on-screen. For example, if you select a line, you can pick a new point for the line's start point.

You can close the Properties window by clicking its Close button.

PSETUPIN

Imports a page setup that you saved in another drawing so you don't have to redefine your page setup from scratch.

Command line only

How to use it

For more information on page setups, see the PAGESETUP command.

AutoCAD opens a dialog box, where you can choose the drawing that has that wonderful page setup you are longing for. Then you see the Import User Defined Page Setups dialog box, which lists the saved page setups in that drawing. Choose one or more and click OK.

To use a page setup that you've imported, open the Page Setup dialog box. In the Page Setup Name drop-down list, choose the page setup. Click OK.

PSPACE

Switches to paper space. This concept enables you to create floating viewports to show various views of your drawing as well as to set up a title block and border and, in general, prepare a layout for plotting.

How to use it

Use PSPACE to work on your layout, for example, by creating or moving floating viewports or changing their layer. You can also add a title block and text in paper space.

If you are on a layout tab in model space, you can switch to paper space by double-clicking any place that's not inside a viewport. *See also* MSPACE and MVIEW.

PURGE

Removes unused blocks, layers, dimension styles, text styles, multi-line styles, shapes, and linetypes from the drawing database, reducing the size of the drawing.

Menu: Choose File⇨Drawing Utilities⇨Purge.

How to use it

You can choose a specific option to purge, or choose the All option to get rid of everything. AutoCAD lists the names of unused layers, blocks, and so on. AutoCAD then asks, Verify each name to be purged? [Yes/No] <Y>. Type **n** @e to purge everything without having to review each item. Otherwise, for each item that you want to purge, press Enter.

 You might have to use PURGE more than once to get to nested blocks and so on.

QDIM

 Creates a series of dimensions, one after the other.

Toolbar: On the Dimension toolbar, choose Quick Dimension.

Menu: Dimension⇨QDIM.

How to use it

Choose the objects you want to dimension. They should be related, such as a group of circles for which you want to create radius

dimensions or a group of lines for which you want to create continuous dimensions. Now right-click and choose one of the following types of dimensions:

✦ Continuous

✦ Staggered

✦ Baseline

✦ Ordinate

✦ Radius

✦ Diameter

✦ Datum Point (sets a new point for baseline or ordinate dimensions)

Now all you do is place the dimension line. AutoCAD displays an image of the proposed dimension so you can get an idea of what it will look like when you finish it. Pick a point and — lickety split — you have a whole bunch of dimensions.

More stuff

You can also use the Edit option to edit existing quick dimensions. AutoCAD prompts you for a dimension point to remove, or you can use the Add option to add a point. AutoCAD then recalculates the dimension.

QLEADER

Creates a leader and leader text. (A *leader* usually points to an object and contains explanatory text.)

Toolbar: On the Dimension toolbar, choose Quick Leader.

Menu: Dimension⇨Leader.

How to use it

To make drawing leaders really quick, you first need to use the Settings option, which opens the Leader Settings dialog box. This part is slow, not quick, but if you're lucky you have to do this only occasionally. This dialog box has three tabs:

✦ **Annotation:** You choose the type of text you want, that is, multiline text (MText), an object that you copy from your drawing, a tolerance, a block that you choose, or none. If you choose MText, you can decide whether you want AutoCAD to prompt you for a width for the entire text (so that the text wraps if longer than the width). You can choose to always left justify the annotation and to frame it in a box. You can also reuse the next annotation that you create for subsequent leaders.

✦ **Leader Line & Arrow:** You can create straight line segments or splines. You can specify a maximum number of segments. Use the Arrowhead section to choose an arrowhead type. Use the Angle Constraints section to set the angles for the first and second segments of the leader.

✦ **Attachment:** Use this tab to determine how multiline text is attached to the leader line. You set the attachment separately for text on the left side of the leader and text on the right side. Now you decide what to do when you have more than one line of text — you specify whether the leaderline meets the text at the top of the top line of the text, the bottom of the bottom line of the text, or somewhere in-between.

When you've finished defining your leader, click OK. Bet you never knew how complex a leader could be! You can now draw the leader.

Pick the first leader point. You can keep on picking points up to the maximum defined in the Leader Settings dialog box. Depending on the other settings, AutoCAD prompts you for text or possibly a block or an object to copy. You're finished!

QSAVE

Saves your drawing.

 Toolbar: On the Standard toolbar, click the Save button.

Menu: Choose File⇨Save.

How to use it

AutoCAD saves your drawing to your hard disk. If you haven't named your drawing, QSAVE opens the Save Drawing As dialog box so that you can type a name.

 Use this command a lot. *Not* using this command is *not* safe!

QSELECT

 Quickly creates a selection set by filtering out unwanted objects.

Menu: Tools⇨Quick Select.

Shortcut menu: With no command active, right-click in the drawing area and choose Quick Select.

How to use it

AutoCAD opens the Quick Select dialog box. By default, the filtering process applies to the entire drawing. If you want, click the Select Objects button to select some objects and apply the filter to only those objects.

In the Object Type drop-down list, choose the type of objects you want to include. Be sure to scroll down to see all the available objects. For example, choose Circle to include only circles in the selection set.

From the Properties list, choose the properties you want to include in the selection set. Then choose an operator for that property. For example, choose > Greater Than if you want to set the radius to be more than 3. In the Value box, you type or choose a value for the property. To find only circles with a radius of more than 3, type 3.

Under How to Apply, you can choose to add the objects you defined to a new selection set. That's the usual method. However, in a great new addition, you can choose to exclude the objects from the selection set — that is, you get a select set of all objects except those that match the criteria. You know, it's not politically incorrect to exclude circles from selection sets.

Finally, if you already have objects selected, you can choose to add (append in AutoSpeak) the objects you have defined in your filter to the existing selection set.

Click OK when you're finished to create the select set. Now go and do something with it.

See also the FILTER command for more advanced filtering.

QTEXT

Turns text objects into rectangles to reduce display and plotting time.

Command line only

How to use it

Type **on** or **off.** When you turn on QTEXT (it stands for quick text), text is displayed as just a rectangle around the text location. Then type **regen** and press Enter to see the result.

More stuff

If you leave QTEXT on when you plot, all you get is rectangles, so don't forget to turn it off before you plot! (QTEXT may be useful for a draft plot, however.)

QUIT

Exits AutoCAD.

Menu: Choose File➪Exit.

Click the Close box at the top right of the title bar.

How to use it

If you haven't made any changes to your drawing, AutoCAD throws you out unceremoniously. If you have made changes, for each open drawing AutoCAD reminds you to save your changes before quitting, if you want.

RAY

Creates a line with a starting point that extends to infinity.

Menu: Choose Draw➪Ray.

How to use it

At the Specify start point prompt, pick a start point of the ray. AutoCAD prompts you for a Through point. Specify another point. The ray continues on and on and on. AutoCAD continues to ask you for Through points so that you can make other rays starting from the same point. Press Enter to end the command.

More stuff

Luckily, commands such as ZOOM Extents ignore rays; otherwise, you'd get some unusual results. Also, the PLOT command doesn't expect an infinite-size sheet of paper — it's all a mirage.

RECOVER

Tries to repair a damaged drawing.

Menu: Choose File➪Drawing Utilities➪Recover.

How to use it

Use this command only after you receive some sort of error message, such as the famous AutoCAD FATAL ERROR message. (Don't be alarmed; I've received lots of fatal error messages, and I'm still alive to write this book.) In other words, you can't open the drawing.

Start a new drawing, and use the RECOVER command. AutoCAD opens the Recover Drawing File dialog box. Select the file from the list. AutoCAD starts recovering the drawing, displaying a report on-screen as it works.

More stuff

See also the AUDIT command, which repairs drawings that you can open. Not every drawing can be recovered. If your drawings are important, get in the habit of making backup copies to floppy disks.

 When you can't get into a drawing, you should first go and rename the drawing's *.bak file and any temporary files (auto.sv$) so that they have *.dwg extensions but different file names. You may be able to open one of them. Another trick is to open a spanking new drawing and try to insert the drawing (using INSERT) and then explode it (using the EXPLODE command).

RECTANG

Draws a rectangle using a polyline.

Toolbar: On the Draw toolbar, click the Rectangle button.

Menu: Choose Draw⇨Rectangle.

How to use it

 This command is easy. AutoCAD prompts you for the two corners of the rectangle. Specify two points and — poof! — you have a rectangle. You can use relative coordinates for the second point. For example, if you type @36,20 for the second point, you get a rectangle that's 36 units wide and 20 units high.

More stuff

RECTANG includes options that enable you to chamfer or fillet the rectangle, as well as give it thickness (3D), elevation (3D), or width. *See also* the CHAMER, FILLET, ELEV, and PLINE commands for more information.

REDO

Redoes whatever the preceding U or UNDO command undid.

 Toolbar: On the Standard toolbar, click the Redo button.

Menu: Choose Edit⇨Redo.

How to use it

When you use the command, AutoCAD redoes whatever you undid with the U or UNDO command.

More stuff

 You need to use this command *immediately* after using the U or UNDO command. Go straight to this command; do not pass Go; do not collect $200. See Chapter 5 of *AutoCAD 2000 For Dummies*.

REDRAWALL

Redisplays the drawing, including all the viewports you have have, removing blip marks and wayward pixels left behind by your editing.

 Toolbar: On the Standard toolbar, click the Redraw All button.

Menu: Choose View➪Redraw.

How to use it

Just use the command; AutoCAD obeys.

The REDRAW command (on the command line only) redraws only the current viewport.

REFEDIT

 Enables you to edit an xref or a block from within your current drawing.

 Toolbar: On the Refedit toolbar, click the Edit block or the Xref button.

Menu: Choose Modify➪In-place Xref and Block Edit➪Edit Reference.

How to use it

Select an xref or a block. AutoCAD opens the Reference Edit dialog box. Here you see a preview of the xref or block.

You can choose from two options:

✦ Choose Enable Unique Layer and Symbol Names to display layer, text style, and other names with a prefix of $#$ so you can easily distinguish them from the names in your current drawing.

✦ Choose Display Attribute Definitions for Editing if you are editing a block with attributes and want to be able to edit them.
Editing changes affect only future insertions of the block.

Click OK to close the dialog box. Now select the objects in the reference or block (called nested objects) that you want to edit. When
you press Enter to end the object selection, you may notice that
the objects you are not editing are somewhat faded. Do not be
alarmed — this is normal! AutoCAD also opens the Refedit toolbar,
which contains the commands you need to finish the process.

You now have the usual command-line prompt and can use any
commands you want to edit the object or objects you have
selected.

Use the Refedit toolbar as follows:

✦ Choose Add Objects to Working Set to select additional objects
for editing. (You can also use the REFSET command with the
Add option.)

✦ Choose Remove Objects from Working Set to remove objects
for editing. (You can also use the REFSET command with the
Remove option.)

✦ Choose Discard Changes to Reference to throw away all your
work and keep the block or xref as it was. (You can also use the
REFCLOSE command with the Discard reference changes
option.)

✦ Choose Save Changes Back to Reference to save your changes
and redefine the block or xref. (You can also use the REFCLOSE
command with the Save option.)

AutoCAD opens a small dialog box asking you to confirm your
choice of either saving or discarding changes. Click OK to confirm.

More stuff

See also XREF and BLOCK for more information about xrefs and
blocks. Use in-place editing with care in a networked environment.

REGEN

Regenerates the drawing, recomputes coordinates, and reindexes
the database.

Menu: Choose View⇨Regen.

How to use it

Start the command; AutoCAD obeys.

More stuff

REGEN takes longer than REDRAW; it updates many changes that have taken place since the last time you did a REGEN. Use REGE-NALL (View⇨Regen All) to regenerate all viewports.

REGENAUTO

Manages the way that AutoCAD regenerates drawings.

Command line only

How to use it

Type **on** or **off**. On means that AutoCAD regenerates automatically when needed — but less often than in previous releases of AutoCAD. Sometimes, regeneration is time-consuming (you can use it as an opportunity for a coffee break), so you might want to set the command to off. Thereafter, each time AutoCAD needs to regen, it asks you whether it should proceed. You can type **y** or **n**, but if you say no, AutoCAD wimps out on you and cancels the command.

REGION

Creates a region object, which is a 2D closed area.

 Toolbar: On the Draw toolbar, click the Region button.

Menu: Choose Draw⇨Region.

How to use it

AutoCAD prompts you to select objects. You can select closed polylines, lines, circles, ellipses, and splines. AutoCAD ignores internal objects as best it can and converts your objects to a region, deleting the original objects in the process. You can't use self-intersecting shapes (such as figure 8s).

More stuff

AutoCAD can do certain things with regions that it can't with the original objects. For example, you can use the MASSPROP command to analyze certain properties, and you can hatch them. Finally, you can use INTERSECT, SUBTRACT, and UNION to play around with sets of regions (called *composite regions*).

See also the BOUNDARY command, which can also create regions, and the BHATCH command if you want to hatch a region.

RENAME

Changes symbol names, such as blocks, layers, styles, and views.

Menu: Choose Format⇨Rename.

How to use it

Select the type of object you want to rename from the Named Objects list. The Items box then lists your objects by name. Select the one you named AuntMelda and type her new name in the Rename To text box. Click OK.

More stuff

You can't rename certain standard objects such as layer 0, style STANDARD, and so on. You can rename many objects in the same dialog box that creates them. For example, to rename a layer, click Object Properties⇨Layers, click the layer name, and type the new name.

RENDER

Shades 3D solid or surface objects using lights, scenes, and materials. Gives a semirealistic appearance to your objects.

 Toolbar: On the Render toolbar, click the Render button.

Menu: Choose View⇨Render⇨Render. (No, you're not seeing double.)

How to use it

 Before you render, you usually create lights with the LIGHT command and a scene with the SCENE command. You can, however, render without any preparation; RENDER uses the current view and a puny default light source.

This command opens the Render dialog box. The Rendering Type drop-down list includes AutoCAD Render, Photo Raytrace, and Photo Real. Choose the type of renderer you want:

- ✦ Render is AutoCAD's original renderer. It's the simplest and fastest.

- ✦ Photo Real creates images line by line. It can display bitmap images, create transparent materials, and make shadows based on volume.

- ✦ Photo Raytrace traces rays of light. It's best for generating precise reflections, refraction, and shadows.

The Scene to Render box lists any scenes you defined. The current view is listed as an option. Choose the one you want.

In the Rendering Procedure section, check one of the options if you want. Query for Selections means that AutoCAD asks you to select objects. Use this to test a rendering on one or more objects — this saves rendering time. Choose Crop Window to choose a window to render, also to save rendering time. Choose Skip Render Dialog to render immediately without even opening the dialog box (the next time).

Set the Light Icon Scale to set the size of the icons that represent lights you've inserted into your scene. Use the drawing scale factor so you can see the light icons clearly in your drawing.

Set the Smoothing Angle. The smoothing angle determines the angle at which AutoCAD defines an edge as opposed to a smooth curve. Angles greater than the smoothing angle are considered to be edges and are not smoothed. The default is 45 degrees. A lower angle results in more edges.

The Rendering Options section enables you to select Smooth Shading. This option blends the colors across adjacent surfaces. Choose Apply Materials to use materials you imported from the materials library and attached to objects (see the MATLIB and RMAT commands). Check Shadows to create shadows. You can create shadows only with the Photo Real and Photo Raytrace renderers. Remember that shadows take much longer to render. Check Render Cache to save rendering information in a file. AutoCAD can reuse this information for subsequent renderings, saving time.

Click More Options (as if you wanted more) to get to the AutoCAD Render Options dialog box. The options depend on the type of renderer you've chosen. For example, if you've chosen the plain-vanilla Render, you can choose between two types of rendering: Phong, which results in higher-quality renderings and better highlights, or Gouraud, which results in faster but lower-quality renderings. Click OK.

The Destination section of the Render dialog box selects the location of the rendered image. If you want to see the results, the location must be either Viewport (the default) or Render Window. The Render Window has its own special menu and toolbar, which enable you to open an image file and save the rendered image to it. You also can copy the image to the Windows clipboard. You can render to a file, if you want.

Use the Sub Sampling drop-down box to set the sampling of pixels that AutoCAD renders. The default, 1:1, renders all the pixels. Try a lower ratio for faster or preliminary renderings.

Click Render to render the selected scene.

Redraw the screen to return to your original wireframe display.

More stuff

See also LIGHT, MATLIB, RMAT, RPREF, SAVEIMG, SCENE, and STATS, which are the other commands related to rendering.

REVOLVE

Draws a solid by revolving a 2D object around an axis.

Toolbar: On the Solids toolbar, click the Revolve button.

Menu: Choose Draw➪Solids➪Revolve.

How to use it

First, you need an object to revolve. The object can be any closed polyline, polygon, circle, ellipse, closed spline, donut, or region. The object can't have crossing or intersecting parts. Next, decide what your axis is. You may want to draw a line so that you can select it to specify the axis.

AutoCAD asks you to select objects. You can revolve only one object at a time, so select one object. Next, you need to specify the axis, using the following options:

Start point of axis	The default. Enables you to specify a point; AutoCAD asks for the endpoint of the axis.
Object	Selects an existing line for your axis.
X	Revolves the object around the positive X axis.
Y	Revolves the object around the positive Y axis.

For all options, AutoCAD then asks whether you want to revolve a full circle (360 degrees) or a specified angle. Your answer completes the command.

More stuff

If several lines and arcs make up the shape you want to revolve, you can use REGION to convert them to one object. Alternatively, see the tip under the PEDIT command for details on turning separate lines and arcs into a polyline.

REVSURF

Draws a surface by revolving a line, an arc, a circle, or a polyline around an axis.

Toolbar: On the Surfaces toolbar, click the Revolved Surface button.

Menu: Choose Draw⇨Surfaces⇨Revolved Surface.

How to use it

First, you need a *path curve,* which means a line, an arc, a circle, or a polyline — this is the object that REVSURF revolves to create the 3D surface. The path curve doesn't have to curve; it can be made up of straight-line segments. Next, you need an object to be your axis (a line or a polyline). Create those first (that's the hard part) and then use the command. AutoCAD prompts you to select a path curve and then the axis of revolution.

Now you need to supply the start angle (the default is 0) and the included angle (the default is a full circle).

RMAT

Defines materials and attaches them to objects to render them.

Toolbar: On the Render toolbar, click the Materials button.

Menu: Choose View⇨Render⇨Materials.

How to use it

Before using this command, use the MATLIB command to load materials from a materials library.

RMAT opens the Materials dialog box. On the left is a list of available materials, which always includes the *GLOBAL* default material. In the middle is a preview box for looking at your beautiful materials.

Defining a material

To create a new material from scratch, choose a type of material from the drop-down box beneath the New button. Choose granite, marble, or wood if you want your new material to look like granite, marble, or wood. Otherwise, choose Standard. Click New. The New Standard (or Granite or Marble or Wood) Material dialog box opens. Type a name for your material. On the left of the dialog box are the attributes you need to define. (They vary according to the type of

material you chose — the main attributes are listed next.) Select these options one at a time and, for each option, complete the Value and Color settings in the center of the dialog box.

Color/Pattern	Sets the diffuse color — the base color that the object reflects. Value sets the intensity of the color. To set color, you must deselect the By ACI button. If you choose a bitmap at the bottom of the dialog box, you define a pattern instead of a color. (However, if you created a marble material, for example, you choose the stone and vein colors.)
Ambient	Sets the color reflected from ambient light. (See the LIGHT command.) The default value is usually a good guide.
Reflection	At the higher value, creates a shiny effect.
Roughness	Relates to the Reflection value. You set only the value — no color. A higher roughness setting produces a bigger reflection highlight.
Transparency	At the highest value, creates a material that is completely transparent. A middle value creates a translucent material.
Refraction	*Refraction* is the bending of a light wave when it passes through an object. Use refraction only in the Photo Raytrace renderer when you have a transparent (or translucent) material. A higher value increases the refraction.
Bump Map	Makes your material look bumpy. You use the bottom part of the dialog box to choose the bump map and for bump map settings.

 Instead of creating a material from scratch, click Modify to change an existing material. Be sure to save it to a different name to preserve your original material.

Or click Duplicate to make a copy of a material and then modify it. The New Standard Material dialog box (or one just like it) opens. Type a new name and make any changes you want.

To see the results, choose Sphere or Cube from the drop-down box under the Preview button. Then click Preview. Continue to fool around with the controls until you like what you see; then click OK to return to the Materials dialog box.

Attaching a material

Now comes the important part: Attaching your new material to an object. Choose your new material from the Materials list and click Attach. Back at your drawing, you can select an object.

You also can attach materials by clicking ACI (AutoCAD Color Index), which opens the (take a deep breath) Attach by AutoCAD Color Index dialog box, where you select a material and an ACI color. Preview displays the selected material. Attach attaches the selected material to the color. Detach detaches the selected material from its color.

Finally, you can attach materials by layer. Click By Layer to open the Attach by Layer dialog box, which works the same way as the Attach by AutoCAD Color Index dialog box. Suppose that you want to attach a material you created a while ago; you've forgotten its name but know that you attached it to another object. Click the Select button, and pick the object in your drawing. AutoCAD returns you to the Materials dialog box, with the material selected.

Choose Detach to detach a material from an object.

See also the RENDER and MATLIB commands.

ROTATE

Rotates objects around a point.

 Toolbar: On the Modify toolbar, click the Rotate button.

Menu: Choose Modify⇨Rotate.

How to use it

The default way to rotate objects is the simplest. Select an object. Specify a base point around which the object rotates. Type a rotation angle (this angle is relative to the object's current position). You also can pick a point to indicate the angle — move the cursor, and the drag copy of the object moves.

You can also right-click and choose the Reference option, which prompts you for a reference angle and a new angle. You can use this method to specify an absolute rotation or to align an object with other objects in your drawing.

ROTATE3D

Rotates objects in 3D space about an axis.

Menu: Choose Modify⇨3D Operation⇨Rotate 3D.

How to use it

Before you start this command, you want to have in mind the axis for rotation. It may help to draw a line so that you can select it.

First, select the objects you want to rotate. Next, the command offers you several options for defining the rotation axis:

2points	Enables you to specify two points on the axis.
Axis by object	Selects a line, a circle, an arc, or a 2D polyline segment. If you select a line or a straight polyline segment, the selected object becomes the axis. If you pick a circle, an arc, or an arc polyline segment, an imaginary line going through the object's center and exiting it perpendicularly becomes the axis.
Last	Uses the preceding axis of rotation.
View	Aligns the axis with the viewing direction and passing through a point that you select.
X, Y, or Z axis	Aligns the axis with the X, Y, or Z axis and passes through a point that you select.

After you define your axis (didn't I tell you that it would be easiest to draw a line and select it?), type the rotation angle or use the Reference option to specify a reference angle and a new angle as you would for the ROTATE command.

RULESURF

Draws a ruled surface mesh between two objects.

Toolbar: On the Surfaces toolbar, click the Ruled Surface button.

Menu: Choose Draw➪Surfaces➪Ruled Surface.

How to use it

Before you use this command, you need to draw two objects that will define the shape of the mesh. You can use points, lines, circles, arcs, or polylines. The two objects must be both open or both closed. AutoCAD prompts you to select the two defining curves (even though they can be straight). Then AutoCAD creates the surface.

More stuff

If the objects are open, such as lines, where you pick the objects matters. If the pick points are on the same end of the two objects, the ruled lines start from the side where you picked and go straight across. If the pick points are on opposite ends of the two objects, the ruled lines cross from one end of the first object to the other end of the second object, creating a self-intersecting mesh. (Well, you have to try it.)

SAVE

Saves the drawing.

Command line only

How to use it

This command has pretty much been superseded by QSAVE, which is available on the Standard toolbar and the File menu.

SAVEAS

Saves a drawing under a new or different name or in a different format.

Menu: Choose File⇨Save As.

How to use it

This command opens the Save Drawing As dialog box. Type a new name in the File name text box. You can also use the Save as type drop-down list to save the drawing in Release 14/LT 98/LT 97 or Release 13/LT 95 format. You can save your drawing in one of several DXF formats (down to Release 12) if you need to share it with someone who has a different CAD program. You can also save the file as a template.

SAVEIMG

Saves a rendered image to a file.

Menu: Choose Tools⇨Display Image⇨Save.

How to use it

AutoCAD opens the Save Image dialog box.

Select the type of file you want to create. Your choices are BMP, TGA, and TIFF. If you chose TGA or TIFF, click Options if you want to specify compression options.

In the Portion box, you can specify a portion of the image to save. Pick the lower-left and upper-right points. The result are reflected in the Offset and Size boxes. Offset is the X and Y distance (in pixels) from the lower-left corner of the Portion box. Size is the X and Y pixels of the area that you selected.

A handy Reset button enables you to reset the image to its original state.

More stuff

If you've rendered to a Render Window, you can choose File⇨Save from the Render Window menu. This method saves the rendering in the BMP format.

SCALE

Changes the size of objects.

Toolbar: On the Modify toolbar, click the Scale button.

Menu: Choose Modify⇨Scale.

How to use it

AutoCAD prompts you to select objects. Then you specify a base point; the object is scaled from that point. Next, type a scale factor. A factor of 2 doubles the size of the object; a factor of .25 reduces the object to one-quarter size.

You also can use the Reference option by right-clicking and choosing Reference after you specify a base point. Specify a reference length and a new length.

SCENE

Creates, changes, and deletes *scenes*, which are like views but include lighting effects. They're used for rendering.

Toolbar: On the Render toolbar, click the Scenes button.

Menu: Choose View⇨Render⇨Scene.

How to use it

Before using this command, you usually use the VIEW command to create a view and the LIGHT command to add lights to a drawing. The SCENE command puts a view and lights together and names them so that you can use them for rendering.

AutoCAD opens the Scenes dialog box, which simply lists defined scenes. The dialog box has three options: New, Modify, and Delete.

New	Opens the New Scene dialog box to create a new scene. Under Scene Name, type a new name. The Views section lists views. Select a view or *CURRENT* from the list. Under Lights, select as many lights as you want or *ALL*.
Modify	Enables you to select one of the scenes from the Scenes dialog box, and click Modify. The Modify Scene dialog box opens. You can change the scene name, view, and lights.
Delete	Enables you to select one of the scenes from the Scenes dialog box, and click Delete. At the prompt, click OK to confirm the deletion.

More stuff

Would you believe that you can have up to 500 lights in a scene? Talk about blinding!

SECTION

Creates a region from the intersection of a plane and solids. This region is the cross-section of the solid.

 Toolbar: On the Solids toolbar, click the Section button.

Menu: Choose Draw⇨Solids⇨Section.

How to use it

First, you need a solid to select. You also can have an object to select for the intersecting plane, or you can specify the plane during the command.

AutoCAD prompts you to select objects. If you select more than one solid, you get more than one region. Then choose options for defining the intersecting plane:

3points	Enables you to specify three points in the plane.
Object	Selects a circle, an ellipse, an arc, a 2D spline, or a 2D polyline segment.
Zaxis	Enables you to specify a point on the plane, and then specify a point on the Z axis of the plane, which means a point exiting the plane perpendicularly. This vector is called a *normal*.
View	Enables you to specify a point in the view plane.
XY, YZ, or ZX plane	Aligns the sectioning plane with the XY, YZ, or ZX plane. You simply pick a point in the plane.

SELECT

Puts selected objects in the *Previous selection set* so that you can use the set with the next command.

Command line only

How to use it

You select objects with the SELECT command just as you do for any other command that asks you to select objects. Here, for the record, is the complete, exhaustive list of the ways you can select objects. After you select the objects, press Enter to complete the command; then you start any editing command. Type **p** (for previous) to select all the objects.

AUto	The default, so you probably are already using it. Enables you to click an object to select it, and click any blank space to start the first corner of a window, regular (see Window) or crossing.
Add	The default. Enables you to select an object to add it to the selection set, so you get more and more objects.
ALL	Selects all objects in the drawing except ones on frozen or locked layers. Includes objects on layers that are turned off.
BOX	Enables you to select two diagonal points that define a box. If the first point you select is on the left and the second is on the right, this option is the same as Window. If you pick points from right to left, this option is the same as Crossing. Auto includes this option.
Crossing	Enables you to select two diagonal points that define a box or a window, starting from the right and ending on the left. Any objects inside the box or crossing its perimeter are selected.
CPolygon	Similar to Crossing, but instead of picking two points, you pick a whole bunch of them, in a sort of roundabout fashion, to create a polygon. Any objects inside the box or crossing its perimeter are selected.
Fence	Similar to CPolygon but open — a bunch of continuous lines that select any object they cross.
Group	Selects objects in a named group. You have to type the name. (See the GROUP command.)
Last	Selects the most recently created object.
Multiple	Enables you to select objects without highlighting them during the selection process.
Previous	Selects the same objects that were selected in the last selection process. The SELECT command uses this option. The Previous option enables you to use several commands on the same set of objects. The Previous selection set gets lost if you erase objects or switch between paper and model space

(continued)

Remove	Removes whatever you select from the selection set instead of adding it. (This situation can get confusing.) Use the Add option when you finish removing and want to start adding.
SIngle	Selects only one object. AutoCAD doesn't prompt you to select any more objects.
Undo	Cancels the most recent selection.
Window	Enables you to pick two diagonal points; everything that's completely inside the box's perimeter is selected.
WPolygon	Same as CPolygon, except selects only objects completely inside the polygon.

SETVAR

Sets values for system variables.

Menu: Choose Tools⇨Inquiry⇨Set Variable.

How to use it

System variables store all sorts of information about your drawing and about AutoCAD in general. Usually, you can use a regular command rather than a system variable. When you use DIMSTYLE to create a dimension style, for example, you affect a whole slew of system variables that relate to dimensions.

Occasionally, you may need to change a system variable directly. If you know the variable's name, you don't even need the SETVAR command. Type the variable name and press Enter; then type the new value and press Enter to end the command.

You can get a list of all the variables by typing **?** at the first prompt. See Part III for a list of useful system variables.

SHADEMODE

Creates a shaded image 3D object. The shading persists until you turn it off.

Menu: Choose View⇨Shade.

How to use it

Choose one of the options on the submenu:

✦ 2D Wireframe: Turns shading off. All objects are displayed as wireframes.

♦ 3D Wireframe: Turns shading off. All objects are displayed as wireframes. AutoCAD displays a cute, colorful 3D UCS icon, instead of the usual, boring UCS icon.

♦ Hidden: Similar to using the HIDE command.

♦ Flat Shaded: Shades objects with an even shading between polygon faces. If you have applied a material to the object, AutoCAD displays it. (You might have to configure your graphics display. To do so, choose Properties on the System tab of the Options dialog box, and then check Enable Materials.)

♦ Gouraud Shaded: Shades objects gradually between polygon faces, resulting in a more realistic look. If you have applied a material to the object, AutoCAD displays it. (You may need to configure your graphic display. To do so, choose Properties on the System tab of the Options dialog box, and then check Enable Materials.)

♦ Flat Shaded, Edges On: Like flat shading, but you also see the wireframe display. Helpful when you want to edit objects with shading on.

♦ Gouraud Shaded, Edges On: Like Gouraud shading, but you also see the wireframe display. Helpful when you want to edit objects with shading on.

SKETCH

Draws freehand line segments.

Command line only

How to use it

This command is for you artists out there. When you start the command, AutoCAD prompts you for a *record increment* — the length of the line segments. The smaller the increment, the smoother the line. SKETCH draws temporary lines and adds them permanently when you exit. This command gives you a little menu that contains the following options:

Pen	Typing **p** raises and lowers the imaginary sketching pen. When the pen is lowered, you can sketch. Raise the pen to stop sketching. When you start this command, the pen is down, so you just press your left mouse button and move the mouse around to sketch.
eXit	Exits sketch mode and gives you a report on how many lines you sketched.

(continued)

Quit	Erases all the temporary lines. You use this option a lot, because it's darn hard to get anything to look good with this command. So quit and try again.
Record	Makes the temporary lines permanent and gives you a report on the number of lines recorded.
Erase	Erases any portion of a temporary line and raises the pen (if it's down).
Connect	Lowers the pen to continue sketching from the end of the last sketched line.
. (period)	Lowers the pen, draws a straight line from the end of the last sketched line to your current position, and raises the pen again. (You have to see this to understand it.)

More stuff

You won't use this command often, but it's fun. You can use the command when you want to draw squiggly lines — in a map, for example. (Remember Etch-a-Sketch?)

SLICE

Slices a solid with a plane. You can retain one or both sides of the sliced solid.

Toolbar: On the Solids toolbar, click the Slice button.

Menu: Choose Draw⇨Solids⇨Slice.

How to use it

First, you need a solid object to slice. You also may want to have some object that you can select to define the slicing plane.

Select the solid. Then specify the plane by using one of the following methods:

3points	Enables you to specify three points in the plane.
Object	Selects a circle, ellipse, arc, 2D spline, or 2D polyline segment.
Zaxis	Enables you to specify a point in the plane. Then you specify a point on the Z axis of the plane, which means a point that exits the plane perpendicularly. This is called a *normal*.
View	Enables you to specify a point in the view plane.
XY, YZ, ZX	Aligns the sectioning plane with the XY, YZ, or ZX plane. You just pick a point in the plane.

AutoCAD then prompts you for a point on the desired side of the plane. If you pick a point, the part of the solid on that side of the plane is retained. The rest of the solid goes poof! Right-click and choose Keep both sides to — you guessed it — keep both sides.

SNAP

Snaps the cursor to set intervals. This command is useful for drawing to exact points.

Command line only

To turn SNAP on and off, click SNAP in the status bar.

How to use it

To change the snap spacing, rotation, style, and type, use the DSET-TINGS command or the SNAP command at the command line. For snap spacing, just type a number. Typing **.25**, for example, makes the cursor jump to every quarter-unit.

Use the Aspect option when you want the X and Y spacing to be different. Rotation rotates the crosshairs and snap points from a base point. Specify the base point and rotation angle. Style enables you to change to isometric mode. (See the ISOPLANE command.)

SNAP has a new Type option: Polar. You can set the type to Grid, which snaps the cursor along a rectangular grid — the familiar type of snap. The Polar type snaps the cursor to the set interval along the polar tracking angles.

See also the DSETTINGS command for more information on snap and polar tracking settings. Right-click the SNAP or POLAR button on the status bar and choose Settings.

SOLID

Draws filled 2D polygonal objects.

Toolbar: On the Surfaces toolbar, click the 2D Solid button.

Menu: Choose Draw⇨Surfaces⇨2D Solid.

How to use it

If fill is off, first use the FILL command to turn fill on. SOLID prompts you to specify two points. Now comes the tricky part. At the prompt for the third point, pick a point diagonally opposite the second point that you picked (this is *not* ring-around-a-rosy). If you want a triangle, press Enter at the prompt for a fourth point.

If you want more than three sides, pick a fourth point diagonally opposite from your first point. Again, you can end here by pressing Enter, but AutoCAD keeps prompting you for third and fourth points so that you can expand your polygon in new and unusual shapes.

More stuff

Picking points around a rosy — that is, around the perimeter of your polygon — results in the infamous AutoCAD bow tie that all of us have created too many times in the past. Try it, and join the family of frustrated AutoCAD users!

SOLIDEDIT

Edits solid objects, especially their faces and edges.

Toolbar: All the buttons on the Solids Editing toolbar

Menu: Choose Modify⇨Solids Editing⇨All the submenu items.

How to use it

SOLIDEDIT introduces an entirely new feature of AutoCAD 2000 — the editing of solids. For some reason, they decided to put every feature into one huge command, making it rather unmanageable, but here goes.

Editing faces

For all the options, you need to select one or more faces, which is the hard part. Often, what you pick is not what you get. But keep trying and make liberal use of the Remove option to remove faces you don't want.

The first group of options lets you edit the faces of solids. Here's how to use them:

Extrude	Extrudes a face. Works just like the EXTRUDE command, but on a face. AutoCAD asks you for the height and a taper angle. Instead of a height, you can specify a path by selecting an existing object.
Move	Moves a face or faces on a solid. Works like the MOVE command. Usually used to move a hole or an extruding section of a solid.
Rotate	Rotates a face or faces. Works like the ROTATE command. Usually used to rotate a hole or an extruding section of a solid.
Offset	Offsets faces works like the OFFSET command. Use a positive value to increase the size or volume of the solid (and decrease the size of a hole). Use a negative value to decrease the size or volume of the solid (and increase the size of a hole).

Taper	Tapers faces with an angle. You can taper holes or an entire solid. You pick a base point and a second point to indicate the direction of the taper, and then specify an angle. A positive angle tapers the face in, and a negative angle tapers the face out.
Delete	Deletes faces. Great for removing fillets and chamfers. Just pick the face and it's gone.
Copy	Copies a face or faces. Works like the COPY command. AutoCAD creates a region or a body from the new face, which you can then use to develop another solid.
Color	Sets the color of a face. You select the color using the Select Color dialog box. You can use this to make a face more visible or for attaching a material based on color. (See the RMAT command.)

Each prompt also has an Undo and an Exit option. You'll use these two options a lot!

Editing edges

You can only copy and color edges. When you copy an edge you get a line, an arc, a circle, an ellipse, or a spline, depending on the edge's shape. The prompts are just like those for editing faces.

Editing solids as a whole

Imprinting is like stamping the shape of an object on a 3D solid. It's a strange concept. You can imprint arcs, circles, lines, 2D and 3D polylines, ellipses, splines, regions, bodies (don't ask for an explanation), and 3D solids. Draw the object you want to imprint so that it intersects or lies on the solid. Then select the solid and the object you want to imprint. AutoCAD asks whether you want to delete the source object — meaning the object you are imprinting, not the solid you are imprinting on. Type **y** @e to delete the object and **n** @e to retain it.

You can **separate** solids that have no common volume. You might not realize this, but you can create one solid of separate, untouching solids using the UNION command. These solids are like the Borg in Star Trek; although they look separate, they are one. Just select the solid and AutoCAD separates it.

Shelling carves the inside of a solid so you end up with a thin wall around its outside. It's like carving a drinking glass from a solid piece of marble. You just select the solid and then the face you want to remove. Usually, you want to remove a face; otherwise, you just hollow out the inside of the solid but leave all the faces intact, like a box with its cover on. Finally, you specify the shell offset distance, which is the thickness of the wall. Use a positive value to create a shell to the inside of the current perimeter of the solid, or a negative value to create a shell to the outside.

Cleaning cleans up a solid. Most often, you use this to remove imprinting. AutoCAD also removes redundant edges and vertices and anything else that doesn't seem to be doing anybody any good.

Checking validates the 3D solid object as a valid ACIS solid. (ACIS is the name of the modeling engine used by AutoCAD for solids.) Now you know you can do all sorts of fancy things with your solid.

SPELL

Checks the spelling of text.

Menu: Choose Tools⇨Spelling.

How to use it

Select the text that you want to spell check. The text can be created with TEXT, DTEXT, or MTEXT. AutoCAD opens the Check Spelling dialog box. When AutoCAD finds a misspelled word, it displays the word in the Current word box and suggests alternatives in the Suggestions box. The Context box shows you the phrase in which the misspelled word was found. Here are the options:

Ignore	Leaves that occurrence of the word alone and goes on to the next.
Ignore All	Ignores all occurrences of the word.
Change	Changes that occurrence of the word to whatever is in the Suggestions box.
Change All	Changes all occurrences of the word to whatever is in the Suggestions box.
Add	Adds the word to the current dictionary.
Lookup	Checks the spelling of the word in the Suggestions box.

Click Change Dictionaries to use another spelling dictionary.

SPHERE

Draws a 3D solid sphere.

Toolbar: On the Solids toolbar, click the Sphere button.

Menu: Choose Draw⇨Solids⇨Sphere.

How to use it

If you're looking for a smooth entry into 3D, you're in the right place. AutoCAD makes drawing spheres easy.

First, specify a 3D point for the center of the sphere (X,Y,Z coordinates). Then specify a length for the radius, or right-click and choose Diameter to specify a diameter.

SPLINE

Draws a spline curve. A spline uses a series of points as a frame to create a smooth curve.

 Toolbar: On the Draw toolbar, click the Spline button.

Menu: Choose Draw⇨Spline.

How to use it

Specify two or more points to define the spline. Press Enter when you finish picking points. Although the prompt doesn't tell you, you can type **undo** after any point to remove it.

The SPLINE command now demands that you enter start and end tangent points to define the angle of the start and end of the spline. (No, I'm not going to give you a course in geometry here.) Move the cursor to see the result on the curve. You can press Enter and have AutoCAD calculate default tangents.

You can right-click and choose Close to close the spline. You can choose the Fit Tolerance option and enter a value in units. A 0 tolerance means that the spline has to go through each point; a bigger number gives the spline more leeway, resulting in a less accurate but smoother curve.

More stuff

At the first prompt, you also can choose the Object option. Then pick a 2D or 3D polyline on which you used the Spline option. SPLINE converts the polyline to a spline and deletes the polylines.

 The technical name for what SPLINE draws is a quadratic or cubic nonuniform rational B-spline (or NURBS) curve. Sounds NURBY to me.

SPLINEDIT

Edits splines.

 Toolbar: On the Modify II toolbar, click the Edit Spline button.

Menu: Choose Modify⇨Spline.

How to use it

To understand editing splines, you need to understand fit points and control points:

- ✦ Fit points are the points you picked when you created the spline.

- ✦ Control points are points that AutoCAD determines mathematically to display the spline.

Now, select the spline. The control points are shown as grips. Notice that they're not on the spline. Here are your options:

Fit Data	Shows your fit points, which are on the spline unless you specified a tolerance greater than 0. This option doesn't appear if you purged the fit data (how dare you?), refined the spline, or moved a control point. If the option appears and you choose it, the grips now show the fit points instead of the control points and you get the following submenu:	
	Add	Adds fit points to a spline. You select a fit point and then a new point. The new point goes between the selected point and the next point.
	Close	Closes the spline.
	Open	Opens a closed spline.
	Delete	Deletes a selected fit point.
	Move	Moves fit points. You get a sub-submenu (are you following me?) that enables you to move to the next or preceding point, select a point, exit the sub-submenu (whew!), or pick a new location for the fit point that you selected.
	Purge	Removes the spline's fit data from the drawing database. AutoCAD can create the spline with only the control points.
	Tangents	Specifies new start and end tangents. (See the SPLINE command.)
	toLerance	Sets a new tolerance. Type **L** to get this option. (*See* the SPLINE command.)
	eXit	Leaves the submenu and returns to the original prompt.
Close	Same as Close in the submenu.	
Open	Same as Open in the submenu.	
Move Vertex	Oh no, another submenu. The Next and Previous options enable you to move from vertex to vertex. After you have it, pick the new location. Alternatively, you can choose Select Point to pick the vertex you want to move and then pick its new location. You also have the eXit option (thank goodness).	

Refine	Offers you suboptions so that you can add control points, elevate the spline's order (they mean allowing for more control points — I suppose that makes the spline more orderly), and give more weight to certain control points, which is sort of like increasing their gravitational pull on the spline.
rEverse	Reverses the spline's direction.
Undo	Cancels the last editing operation. (You need this option often, I assure you.)
eXit	Ends the SPLINEDIT command.

STATUS

Lists the status of drawing statistics and modes.

Menu: Choose Tools⇨Inquiry⇨Status.

How to use it

This command lists the status of many of the commands you use for setting up your drawing, the current layer, color, and linetype, the number of objects in the drawing, and some systemwide information such as free disk space, memory, and swap file space. You can use it for troubleshooting, to share the information with a colleague, or just to waste time.

STRETCH

Stretches objects.

Toolbar: On the Modify toolbar, click the Stretch button.

Menu: Choose Modify⇨Stretch.

How to use it

AutoCAD prompts you to select objects. You *must* use the crossing window or CPolygon method of selection. Any line, arc, or polyline that *crosses* the selection window is stretched by moving the endpoints that lie *inside* the window. Enclose the endpoints of the objects that you want stretched in the crossing window, and you come out okay. Objects completely inside the window are just moved.

Like the MOVE command, STRETCH asks you for a base point and a second point of displacement.

If you want to stretch without changing the angle, turn on ORTHO or use polar tracking.

STYLE

Manages text styles.

Menu: Choose Format⇨Text Style.

How to use it

AutoCAD opens the Text Style dialog box. In the Style Name section, choose a style from the drop-down list to make that style current. You can also delete or rename a style. To create a new style, click New and name the new style. Click OK. To modify an existing style, choose it from the list.

Use the rest of the dialog box to define a new style or redefine an existing style.

In the Font section, choose a font, choose a style such as bold or italic (if supported by the font you chose), and then set a height. If you set the height to 0, AutoCAD prompts you for the height each time you use the text style, and you can vary the height if you want.

In the Effects section, choose Backwards, Upside-down, or Vertical if you want those effects. The Vertical option (like text going down the spine of a book) appears only for the fonts that support it.

Now specify a width factor. A value of 1 is normal. A larger number gives you fat (expanded) text; a smaller number (between 0 and 1) gives you skinny (condensed) text.

For the obliquing angle, type an angle. Angles between 0 and 15 are useful for that italic look.

The Preview box shows you the beautiful style you've created. Use the Preview text box to type whatever you want. Click Preview and AutoCAD shows you that text in the Preview box.

Click Apply to apply the style to all text in your drawing that uses that style. Then click Close to close the dialog box.

More stuff

AutoCAD comes with one style, called STANDARD. This style is boring, so create your own. All text commands offer you an opportunity to change the style before you start writing your novel.

 See Chapter 10 of *AutoCAD 2000 For Dummies.*

STYLESMANAGER

Opens the Plot Styles folder, where you can add or edit plot style tables and plot styles. A plot style is an object property (such as color or linetype) that controls how objects are plotted, including color, linetype, lineweight, line fill, and screening. Plot styles are stored in plot style tables.

Menu: Choose File⇨Plot Style Manager.

How to use it

The Add-a-Plot-Style-Table Wizard helps you create a new plot style table. You can also edit existing plot style tables by double-clicking them to open the Plot Style Table Editor.

Creating a new plot style table

To create a new plot style table, double-click the Add-a-Plot-Style-Table Wizard icon. You can choose to start from scratch, use an existing plot style table as a basis for the new one, use a pen table from a Release 14 configuration (.cfg) file, or import pen table properties from existing .pcp (Release 13) or .pc2 (Release 14) plot configuration files.

Next, you choose the type of plot style table you want to create:

✦ Color-dependent tables contain 255 plot styles, one for each color, and create a file with the extension .ctb. You can't add or delete plot styles, but you can edit them. Plotting properties are based on object color, as they were in previous releases of AutoCAD. Use color-dependent tables to maintain compatibility with existing color-based settings.

✦ Named tables start with one plot style, called Normal, and create a file with the extension .stb. You then add your own plot styles to the table with the plotting properties you want. Plotting properties are independent of color; you can attach a plot style to a layer or to an individual object.

After you save a drawing in AutoCAD 2000 format, its plot style table type is etched in stone. You can, however, change the type of table you use for new drawings you create as well as for earlier release drawings that you open in AutoCAD 2000 format and save — choose Tools⇨Options and click the Plotting tab. If you want to keep older drawings in color-dependent table mode but use the named table mode for new drawings, you should use the color-dependent setting, open *all* your older drawings in AutoCAD 2000, save them, and only then switch to named table mode.

The wizard asks you to give your plot style table a file name. On the last screen of the wizard, click Plot Style Table Editor to open your new plot style table and give it the settings you want. You can also check Use this plot style table for new and pre-AutoCAD 2000 drawings if you want this new plot style table to be your default.

Using the Plot Style Table Editor

Use the Plot Style Table Editor to specify plot styles in a plot style table that you have just created or to edit existing plot style tables. The figure shows the Plot Style Table Editor's table view for a named plot style table. The table view lets you see several plot styles side by side. The form view concentrates on one plot style at a time and uses a form layout to specify the plot style properties.

Here are your options when you define a plot style:

Color	Enables you to change the color used when an object is plotted.
Dithering	Dithering is a way to approximate intermediate colors using dot patterns. Some plotters (for example, pen plotters) do not support dithering. Dithering can make thin lines look funny because they might look as if they are made up of dots, instead of being continuous. Dithering also makes light colors dimmer, because of the spaces between the dots. The advantage of dithering is that you can approximate the look of more colors than those available in the AutoCAD Color Index.

Convert to Grayscale	Converts all colors to shades of gray, if your plotter supports grayscale printing.
Use Assigned Pen #	Applies to pen plotters only, to specify a pen to use for objects that use this plot style. You can't set this value if the plot style color is set to Use Object Color, or if you are editing a color-dependent plot style table.
Virtual Pen #	Applies to non-pen plotters that can simulate a pen plotter, using the concept of virtual pens. For many of these plotters, you can then program the pen's width, fill pattern, color/screening, and other characteristics on the front panel of the plotter. Therefore, if the plotter is configured to use virtual pens, AutoCAD ignores any other settings of the plot style and uses only the settings assigned by the plotter to the virtual pen. To configure a plotter for virtual pens, use the Vector Graphics setting on the Device and Document Settings tab of the Plotter Configuration Editor. See the PLOT-TERMANAGER command.
Screening	Specifies how much ink the plotter uses when plotting. A setting of 100 plots the color at full force. A setting of 0 plots nothing — you just see a white sheet of paper. You can set anything in-between.
Linetype	By default, AutoCAD uses the linetype assigned to the object.
Adaptive Adjustment	Adjusts the scale of the linetype to complete the linetype pattern so that a line doesn't end in the middle of a pattern. Turn it off if accurate linetype scale is important to you. Turn it on if you'd rather see complete linetype patterns.
Lineweight	By default, AutoCAD uses the lineweight assigned to the object (either directly or through the object's layer). You can choose another lineweight if you want.
Line End Style	If you use thick lineweights, enables you to specify how the ends of lines look. By default, AutoCAD uses the object's end style, but you can specify one of the following: butt, square, round, or diamond.
Line Join Style	If you use thick lineweights, enables you to specify how lines are joined where they meet. By default, AutoCAD uses the object's join style, but you can assign one of the following: miter, bevel, round, or diamond.
Fill Style	Enables you to change an object's fill, usually created by hatching. The default is to use the object's fill style, but you can choose one of the following: solid, checkerboard, crosshatch, diamonds, horizontal bars, slant left, slant right, square dots, or vertical bar.

When you are finished with the plot style, click Save and Close. If you entered the Plot Style Table Editor from the wizard, click Finish to close that as well. You can now use your plot style.

Using plot styles and plot style tables

Now that you have a plot style, how do you use the thing? First, you have to attach a plot style table to the Model tab or one of the layout tabs. In this way, you have the flexibility to attach different plot style tables to a layout to create different plots from the same drawing. To attach a plot style table to an active tab, right-click the tab and choose Page Setup. On the Plot Device tab, choose a plot style table from the Plot Style Table drop-down list. Click OK. For more information, see the PAGESETUP command.

If you are using named plot styles, you can then assign a plot style from within the plot style table to an object or a layer. You can't do this if you are using color-dependent plot style tables because the plot styles are automatically assigned based on the object's color.

To create or edit a layer that uses a plot style, choose Layers from the Object Properties toolbar (the LAYER command). In the Layer Properties Manager dialog box, click the Plot Style property of the layer. In the Select Plot Style dialog box, choose a plot style and click OK. Click OK to close the Layer Properties Manager dialog box. Now every object on that layer uses the plot style you specified. Note that by default, the plot style of a layer is NORMAL.

To change the plot style for an object, select the object and click the Plot Style Control drop-down list on the Object Properties toolbar. Choose the plot style you want to use.

More stuff

To see the result of your plot styles before actual plotting, check Display Plot Styles in the Page Setup dialog box. This works on only a layout tab. You can also click Print Preview on the Standard toolbar.

SUBTRACT

Subtracts the area of one region, or the volume of one solid, from another.

 Toolbar: On the Solid Editing toolbar, click the Subtract button.

Menu: Choose Modify⇨Solid Editing⇨Subtract.

How to use it

First, select the regions or solids you want to subtract from; then select the objects you want to subtract. AutoCAD does the rest.

TABLET

Calibrates a tablet with a paper drawing you want to digitize. Also configures the tablet menu.

Menu: Choose Tools⇨Tablet.

How to use it

Use this command if you use a digitizer.

The first time you use your digitizing tablet, use the CFG option to configure the menu and screen pointing areas (where you draw) of a large tablet. The menu — either the one that AutoCAD provides (look for Acad2000\Sample\Tablet 2000.dwg) or your own customized one — should be attached to the tablet surface. AutoCAD prompts you for the number of tablet menus you want. The menu is divided into areas; you type the number of areas that you're using. If you want to realign the tablet menu areas, type **y** at the next prompt. You need to digitize the points requested for each area. Then AutoCAD asks you how many columns and rows you want for each menu area. In this way, AutoCAD divides each menu area into little boxes, one for each command.

Finally, AutoCAD asks whether you want to respecify the screen pointing area — that's the big box in the middle of the tablet drawing which represents where you draw. Type **y** if you do and digitize the points as requested.

To digitize a paper drawing, first tape the drawing neatly and securely to the digitizer tablet. Then mark three or more points on the paper — perhaps the corners. You can set the lower-left corner as 0,0. Then measure the other points, and write in their coordinates relative to 0,0. If the drawing represents something big like a building, use real-life coordinates. You'll need these coordinates later.

Use the CAL option to calibrate the tablet area with your drawing. Then use the ON option to turn the tablet on. When you finish, turn the tablet off to return to regular drawing mode.

To calibrate the tablet area, type **CAL**. AutoCAD prompts you to digitize the first point. With your puck, pick one of the points that you marked on the paper. AutoCAD prompts you for the point's coordinates. (I told you that you'd need those coordinates.) AutoCAD keeps prompting you for points and their coordinates. You can enter as many points as you want.

Depending on how many points you entered, AutoCAD may provide a very esoteric table that relates to various types of transformations, called Orthogonal, Affine, and Projective. In most cases, you should use Orthogonal. If you don't like the result, see the AutoCAD command reference documentation. (This information is not the stuff of a Quick Reference.)

Use the ON and OFF options to turn the tablet on and off. When the tablet is on, the entire digitizer can be used for digitizing a drawing. When the tablet is off, you use just the small drawing area to draw and the rest for menus. You can usually press Ctrl+T to toggle the tablet on and off.

TABSURF

Draws a 3D tabulated surface, based on a curve and a direction (called a *vector*).

 Toolbar: On the Surfaces toolbar, click the Tabulated Surface button.

Menu: Choose Draw⇨Surfaces⇨Tabulated Surface.

How to use it

You need to select the *path curve*, which defines the shape of the surface, and a *direction vector*, which specifies the direction in which the shape will be extruded. Draw these objects before using the command.

AutoCAD prompts you for a path curve and a direction vector. You select objects for each of these items. The path curve can be a line, an arc, a circle, an ellipse, a polyline, or a spline. The direction vector must be a line or an open polyline. AutoCAD creates the surface.

More stuff

For the direction vector, AutoCAD ignores any intermediate meandering; it simply considers the beginning and end points. The results of this command are somewhat like those of the EXTRUDE command, except that this command creates a surface and the EXTRUDE command creates a solid. ***See also*** the SURFTAB1 and SURFTAB2 system variables in Part III to control the smoothness of the surface.

TEXT

Creates a line of text. This command works just like DTEXT, so see that command. In AutoCAD 2000, TEXT and DTEXT have been combined so that they both do the same thing. You can use either one on the command line. (Why type that extra *D* if you don't have to?)

TIME

Lists date and time information for a drawing.

Menu: Choose Tools⇨Inquiry⇨Time.

How to use it

The TIME command displays when the drawing was created and last updated. This command also tracks the total editing time minus plotting time (not including time when you worked but didn't save your changes). In addition, you can turn a timer on and off for more customized timing. (Maybe you don't want to charge a customer for correcting a mistake that was your fault.) To turn on the timer, use the ON option; to turn it off, use the OFF option. Reset brings the timer back to 0.

TOLERANCE

Creates geometric tolerances.

 Toolbar: On the Dimension toolbar, click the Tolerance button.

Menu: Choose Dimension⇨Tolerance.

How to use it

To use this command, you have to understand tolerances. (A tolerance specifies how much a manufactured object can deviate from an exact measurement.) AutoCAD creates *feature control frames,* which are little boxes that contain the tolerance information that you choose to put there. The frames are then placed next to your dimensions.

Up pops the Geometric Tolerance dialog box, in which you build your feature control frame. This dialog box allows up to two lines of symbols. You build a line from left to right, as follows:

Sym	Opens the Symbol dialog box. Click the type of tolerance symbol you want. Click OK after you're finished. AutoCAD Help, below the TOLERANCE command, contains a list of all the symbols and what they mean.
Tolerance 1	If you want to start with the diameter symbol, click the box at the left of this column. Then type the tolerance value in the text box. Click the right box to open the Material Condition dialog box. These symbols define conditions that apply to materials that can vary in size. M is for At maximum material condition, L is for At least material condition, and S means Regardless of feature size. Click the option you want and then click OK to return to the Geometric Tolerance dialog box.
Tolerance 2	If you want a second tolerance, create it just as you did the first.
Datum 1	*Datum* refers to a theoretically exact geometrical entity from which you can verify the dimensions of your objects. First, type a reference letter that represents your first datum. Click MC if you want to insert a material condition. This process is the same as the one used in creating the tolerance.
Datum 2	Same procedure as Datum 1.
Datum 3	Same procedure as Datum 1.
Projected Tolerance Zone	Type a height, and click the Projected Tolerance Zone box to put in the Projected Tolerance Zone symbol. Type a datum identifier.

Click OK and AutoCAD prompts you for the tolerance location. Pick a point and AutoCAD inserts it.

TOOLBAR

Shows, hides, and customizes toolbars.

Menu: Choose View⇨Toolbars.

Shortcut menu: Right-click any toolbar and choose Customize.

How to use it

AutoCAD opens the Toolbars dialog box.

Managing toolbars

To show a toolbar, click the name of the toolbar you want to show. To hide a toolbar, uncheck it. Then click Close. You also can select a toolbar and delete it. The Show ToolTips button controls whether the button name appears when you place the mouse on the button.

Unless you have memorized all the buttons, keep this option checked! You can click Large Buttons if the standard ones are too itsy-bitsy for you, but of course, they take up much more of your screen.

You don't need the TOOLBARS command to display or hide toolbars. To hide or display a toolbar, right-click the toolbar and choose it from the list. Another method of hiding a *floating* toolbar (one that floats somewhere in the drawing area and is not *docked* on the edges of the screen) is to click the Close button in the upper-right corner. If the toolbar is docked, you can use a simple (and undocumented) method to hide it — drag it from its border onto the drawing area to float it, and then click the Close button.

To dock a floating toolbar, click the toolbar name and then drag the toolbar to the top, bottom, left side, or right side of the screen. The toolbar changes to fit its new location.

To float a docked toolbar, click the grab bars at one end and then drag the toolbar to the drawing area. You can drag the edges of floating toolbars to morph them into any shape.

Creating a new toolbar

Creating a new toolbar that contains the commands you use most and the ones that are hardest to get to is a great idea. However, use AutoCAD for a while before you do so, keeping a wish list of commands that you wish were more accessible. These commands are the ones you want to put in your new toolbar. From the Toolbars dialog box, click New. Type a toolbar name and menu group. (The menu group is ACAD, unless you've created a custom menu, in which case its name appears.) Then click OK. An empty toolbar of your own creation appears on-screen. Now click Customize to add buttons to your toolbar. Click Categories, and the buttons for that category appear, helping you find the button you want. Drag the button from the dialog box to your new toolbar. You also can copy a button from another toolbar by holding down the Ctrl key while you drag the button to the new toolbar.

You can drag buttons only while the Customize Toolbars dialog box is open.

TORUS

Draws a 3D donut.

 Toolbar: On the Solids toolbar, click the Torus button.

Menu: Choose Draw⇨Solids⇨Torus.

How to use it

First, specify the center with a 3D point. Then type a value for the radius of the torus, that is, the distance from the center to the outside of the torus. Next, type a value for the radius of the tube, which is half the width of the tube. At each radius prompt, you also can right-click, choose Diameter, and then specify a diameter.

TRACE

Draws lines that can have a width.

This command has been mostly superseded by the PLINE command. However, you can extrude traces (but not polylines) to create solids.

TRANSPARENCY

Enables you to create transparent images for image types that support transparent pixels.

 Toolbar: On the Reference toolbar, click the Image Transparency button.

Menu: Choose Modify⇨Object⇨Image⇨Transparency.

How to use it

Select an image object and type **on** or **off**. The default is off. Not all images support transparency.

TRIM

Trims objects at an edge created by another object.

 Toolbar: On the Modify toolbar, click the Trim button.

Menu: Choose Modify⇨Trim.

How to use it

First, select the cutting edge. (You can select more than one edge.) The object that you want to trim will be cut off where it intersects that edge (or those edges). You also can trim the object to where it *would* intersect the cutting edge, if the cutting edge were extended (called an *implied intersection*).

Now select the object to be trimmed. Pay attention — you have to select on the part of object that you want to trim. If you've selected two edges and want the object to be trimmed between them, select the object between the edges. The result is like the BREAK command.

If the edge has only an implied intersection with your object, use the Edge option and then turn on the Extend option before selecting your object. That way, AutoCAD knows to calculate the implied intersection. Be sure to select the object on the side you want to trim.

More stuff

Trimming in 3D is a bit more complicated, as you might expect. Select the cutting edge and then right-click and choose the Projection option. You have three projection choices:

None	Trims objects that intersect with the cutting edge in true 3D (you know — real life on your computer screen).
UCS	Projects on the XY plane of the current user coordinate system (UCS).
View	Projects along the current view plane.

You can use the Edge option for 3D trimming as well.

U

Undoes the last operation.

Toolbar: On the Standard toolbar, click the Undo button.

Menu: Choose Edit⇨Undo.

How to use it

U is one of the nicest, sweetest commands around; you could hug it. Amazingly, you can use this command over and over; AutoCAD undoes every (well, almost every) command until you get to where you were at the beginning of the drawing session. Now *that's* a data-base. Obviously, U cannot undo things such as plotting or saving your drawing. *See also* the UNDO command, which is a more robust version of U.

UCS

Manages the user coordinate system (UCS), which defines where 0,0 is and which way the X, Y, and Z axes point.

 Toolbar: On the Standard toolbar, click the UCS button.

Menu: Choose Tools⇨New UCS.

How to use it

UCS has the following options:

✦ New creates a new UCS. AutoCAD offers suboptions for the various methods of defining a new UCS:

- Origin changes the origin, leaving the axes in the same direction as before.

- Zaxis enables you to define an origin and a point on the positive Z axis. The XY axis is tilted accordingly.

- 3point defines the UCS using three points. The first point is the origin. Then specify any point on the desired X axis. Finally, specify a point on the new Y axis.

- Object uses an object to define the UCS. The results depend on the object. For example, if you pick a point on the circumference of a circle, the origin is the circle's center and the X axis passes through your pick point.

- Face, a new option, asks you to select the face of a solid. You can then move through the possible UCSs using the Next suboption, or flip the UCS around the X axis (the Xflip suboption) or the Y axis (the Yflip suboption).

- View creates a new UCS with the XY plane parallel to your current viewpoint (that is, parallel to your screen). The origin remains unchanged. This option is good for creating text that looks normal on a 3D drawing viewed at an angle. It's not good for much else.

- X rotates the UCS around the X axis. You specify the rotation angle. The origin remains unchanged.

- Y rotates the UCS around the Y axis. You specify the rotation angle. The origin remains unchanged.

- Z rotates the UCS around the Z axis. You specify the rotation angle. The origin remains unchanged. This option can be used in 2D drawings.

✦ Move keeps the direction of the X and Y axes the same but moves the origin. You either specify the new origin or provide the Z depth, which is the positive or negative change in the Z coordinate of the origin.

✦ Orthographic offers six standard UCSs so you don't have to create your own: top, bottom, front, back, left, and right.

✦ Prev brings back, brings back, oh brings back the previous UCS to you, to you. (It's a song!)

✦ Restore returns you to a saved UCS. Type the name or use the ? option to list saved UCSs.

✦ Save saves a UCS. You get to give it a name. Word to the wise — save all useful UCSs.

✦ Del deletes a saved UCS.

 ✦ Apply applies the current UCS to a specified viewport. You can also apply the UCS to all active viewports. In AutoCAD 2000, viewports can each use a different UCS.

✦ ? lists all your UCSs and their properties.

✦ World returns you to the familiar world coordinate system.

More stuff

A UCS sets the direction of the X,Y,Z coordinates. Setting the viewpoint is a separate process, which you perform with DDVPOINT, VPOINT, or 3DORBIT. If you restore a UCS and don't understand why you're looking at things from such a strange angle, use the PLAN command to return to the plan view of the UCS.

See "Creating a user coordinate system (UCS)" in Part I. *See also* the UCSFOLLOW system variable in Part III under "3D."

UCSICON

Manages the UCS icon itself (which usually appears in the lower-left corner of your screen). This command doesn't affect the UCS.

Menu: Choose View⇨Display⇨UCS Icon.

How to use it

The ON option displays the UCS icon; OFF turns it off. Noorigin (no, that's not Norwegian) shows the icon at the lower-left corner of your screen or viewport, no matter where the UCS origin is. The Origin option forces the icon to appear at the origin of the UCS, if there's room.

UCSMAN

Manages UCSs, including restoring saved UCSs, specifying UCS settings, and naming or renaming the current UCS.

Toolbar: Choose Display UCS Dialog on the UCS flyout of the Standard toolbar.

Menu: Choose Tools⇨Named UCS.

How to use it

AutoCAD opens the UCS dialog box, which has three tabs:

✦ Use the Named UCSs tab to choose a named UCS. Click Set Current then click OK. You can also use this tab to save a UCS. First, create the UCS using the UCS command. Then open the UCS dialog box. The current UCS is called Unnamed. Click it once and type a new name. Press Enter and click OK to close the dialog box. Click Details on this tab to get the lowdown on a selected UCS.

✦ Use the Orthographic UCSs to choose one of six standard UCSs: top, bottom, front, back, left, or right. Then click OK.

✦ Use the Settings tab to control the UCS icon. (See the UCSICON command.) You can also decide whether to save a UCS with a specific viewport and whether to go to plan view whenever you change UCSs (the UCSFOLLOW system variable).

More stuff

The VPOINT and DDVPOINT commands set your viewpoint. The UCS command manages the user coordinate system, enabling you to change the origin and direction of the X and Y axes.

UNDO

Undoes commands.

Command line only

How to use it

This command is the big brother or sister (are commands masculine or feminine?) of the U command. Amazingly, AutoCAD retains a database of every action performed during a drawing session so that you can undo commands and return to the pristine state in which you started. Following are the options:

Number	The default. You type a number, and AutoCAD reverses the effect of that many commands. The difference between using this option and using U five times is simply that this option doesn't cause regeneration between each undoing. (Using U five times may or may not cause regeneration, depending on the commands.)
Auto	Undoes any operation performed with a menu used as one command.
Control	Displays a submenu, which contains the options that control the way UNDO works. The All option gives you the full UNDO command. None turns off the U and UNDO commands. (Be careful — being able to undo commands is always nice.) One limits UNDO to reversing one command.
Begin	Groups a series of commands. Use this option when you're trying something new and exciting (but a little dangerous) and you want to be able to undo your work in one fell swoop. Then use U or UNDO 1 to undo the entire group.
End	Ends the group started by BEgin.
Mark	Places a mark at the current location. You then use the Back option to undo back to the mark.
Back	This option can be dangerous. You use Back to undo commands back to the most recent mark. But if you haven't created any marks, watch out. Luckily, AutoCAD displays this prompt: `This will undo everything. OK?` Quickly type **n** — unless you want to undo everything you did today!

More stuff

You can't undo some commands. If you used the LIST command to get information about an object, AutoCAD won't get inside your head and remove the knowledge you've gained. (That's not on my list for a new feature for the next release of AutoCAD, either!)

UNION

Creates one combined region or solid from two or more regions or solids.

Toolbar: On the Solids Editing toolbar, click the Union button.

Menu: Choose Modify⇨Solids Editing⇨Union.

How to use it

This command is how two regions or solids join in holy matrimony (very unexciting, I assure you). First, select the objects. If the objects are regions or solids and can be converted, AutoCAD converts them. All you have to do is watch. (I told you, it's okay; nothing too risqué happens.)

UNITS

Specifies how coordinates and angles are shown, including their precision (the number of places after the decimal point).

Menu: Choose Format⇨Units.

How to use it

AutoCAD opens the Units Control dialog box. First, select the type of units you want to use. Decimal is the default. Engineering and Architectural units show feet and inches, using inches for the drawing unit. Otherwise, a unit can be any measurement you want. Then set the precision you want shown.

In the Angles section, you can choose how you want angle degrees shown and their precision.

In the Drawing Units for DesignCenter blocks, you can set a unit for blocks that you drag in from the DesignCenter. Blocks are then scaled to those blocks. For example, if you choose light years, a block 3 units wide becomes 3 light years wide!

More stuff

Check Clockwise to measure angles so that angles increase in a clockwise direction instead of the standard counterclockwise. Click Direction to change the direction of zero degrees.

VIEW

Creates and restores named views.

 Toolbar: On the Viewpoint flyout of the Standard toolbar, click the Named Views button.

Menu: Choose View⇨Named Views.

How to use it

This command opens the View dialog box. The Named View tab lists the views you've defined and named. A view can be a small, zoomed-in section of your drawing or the whole thing. Naming views helps you get from place to place quickly in a large drawing.

To display a named view, select it from the list, click Set Current, and then click OK. To name the current view, click the word Current, type a new name, and press Enter. Then click OK.

To create a new view, click New to open the New View dialog box. You can name your view and click Current Display (setting up your

display the way you want it before you enter the command helps) or Define Window. If you click Define Window, you have to click the Define View Window button (seems redundant to me). AutoCAD returns you to your drawing momentarily to pick the corners of your view. After you're finished, click OK to return to the View dialog box.

To delete a named view, select it from the list and press the Del key. To rename a view, click its name, type a new name, and press Enter. Try clicking Details to get information describing your view.

More stuff

Views can be in model space or in a paper space layout, but you have to be in the same type of space where the view was created to restore it.

VIEWRES

Sets the resolution for circles and arcs.

Command line only

How to use it

AutoCAD first asks whether you want fast zooms. Just press Enter. This option no longer does anything because you always get fast zooms.

Now comes the reason why you came to this command in the first place. AutoCAD asks you to enter a circle zoom percentage (1 to 20,000) and tells you the current setting. The higher the setting, the smoother your circles and arcs — and the slower AutoCAD's speed. Lower numbers speed things, but circles can look like polygons. Usually, you can get a setting that gives you smooth circles without a noticeable decrease in speed.

If you see a circle that looks like a polygon, don't always assume you have to change VIEWRES. Try a REGEN first.

UPCLIP

Clips existing floating viewports on a layout tab. When you clip a viewport, AutoCAD displays what's only inside the clipped area. Clipping is similar to the concept of cropping a graphic image.

Toolbar: On the Viewports toolbar, click the Click Existing Viewport button.

Menu: Choose Modify⇨Clip⇨Viewport.

Shortcut menu: Select the viewport to clip, right-click in the drawing area, and choose Viewport Clip.

How to use it

Select the viewport you want to clip. You can then select an existing object to use as the clipping boundary or use the Polygonal option to specify points. Pick the first point. You can continue to pick points or use one of these options:

✦ Arc displays a zillion suboptions so you can specify arcs. It's like using the PLINE command.

✦ Close closes the clipping boundary and you're finished.

✦ Length lets you specify a line length. AutoCAD adds a line in the same direction as the previous line segment.

✦ Undo undoes that last segment of the boundary.

You can end the boundary by using the Close option. Otherwise, AutoCAD closes the boundary for you. AutoCAD now displays only those objects within the clipping boundary. You're finally rid of all that extraneous junk you didn't need.

More stuff

See also the MVIEW command to make polygonal floating viewports from scratch, and the VPORTS command to create configurations of floating (on a layout tab) or tiled (on the model tab) viewports.

VPLAYER

Freezes and thaws layers within floating viewports.

Command line only

How to use it

Although this command is accessed directly only on the command line, you can accomplish the same thing in the Layer Properties Manager dialog box — which you access by clicking Layers on the Object Properties toolbar. You may have to expand the dialog box to the right to see the columns you need.

To freeze a layer in the current (active) floating viewport, click its sun icon in the Active VP Freeze column. The sun icon changes to a snowflake. To thaw it, click the snowflake icon.

To freeze a layer for new viewports that you're planning to create, click its sun icon in the New VP Freeze column. To thaw a layer — you guessed it — click its snowflake icon.

Notice that you can also use the Details section (click Show Details if you don't see it) to freeze and thaw layers for the current and new viewports. Just select a layer and check or uncheck the item you want.

More stuff

You can't work with a frozen layer. It's invisible and doesn't plot.

VPOINT

Controls the 3D angle from which you view your drawing.

Menu: Choose View⇨3D Viewpoint⇨VPOINT.

How to use it

The VPOINT command does the same thing as the DDVPOINT command, except VPOINT offers a different conceptualization of 3D space with which to define your viewpoint.

Imagine making two long, crossing cuts in the bottom of a tangerine. Open up the peel and lay it out flat on the table. AutoCAD uses a compass, shown in the figure, to represent the same concept. Just as the center of the tangerine peel was at the top of the tangerine, the center of the compass is the North Pole, equivalent to plan view (the familiar 2D way of looking at things from the top). Because the outer edge of the peel was at the bottom of the tangerine, the outer ring is the South Pole. The whole Southern Hemisphere has been flattened out so that you can see it. The circle between the center and the outer ring is the equator. Anywhere you click inside the inner circle results in a view from above. Anywhere you click between the inner and outer circles results in a view from below.

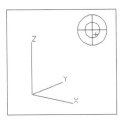

You also have to choose the corner of the Northern or Southern Hemisphere. You do this by paying attention to the crosshairs that go through the circles. Anything below the horizontal crosshair is a front view, just as anything in the bottom half of the peel would have come from the front of the tangerine; anything above the horizontal crosshair is a back view. To the left of the vertical crosshair is a view from the left. To the right of the vertical crosshair is a view from the right. These front, back, left, and right directions are meaningful in relationship to the plan view. The Earth doesn't have a front, back, left, or right. But when you look at things from the top, you think that way.

Along with the compass you see a tripod. You pick your viewpoint on the compass and see the results on the tripod, which is just X,Y,Z axes moving in space. When you pick a point, AutoCAD returns you to your drawing, displaying the new viewpoint.

I hope this explanation helps. Otherwise, create a model that doesn't look the same on all sides, start picking points, and see the results.

More stuff

See also the UCS command for information on creating a user coordinate system. The 3DORBIT command offers another way of creating views from different angles.

VPORTS

Creates configurations of tiled or floating viewports.

Menu: Choose View⇨Viewports.

How to use it

If you are on the Model tab, this command creates tiled viewports. If you are on a layout tab in paper space, this command creates floating viewports. AutoCAD calls the number and layout of viewports *viewport configurations*. Choose New Viewports from the Viewports submenu to open the Viewports dialog box. On the New Viewports tab, you can easily choose a configuration that suits your needs. If you are creating tiled viewports, you can type a name in the New Name text box to save the viewport configuration. You can then use that viewport configuration again either on the Model tab or on a layout tab.

The Preview pane shows the result of your choice. The Apply To drop-down list is active only if you already have some viewports and are creating tiled viewports on the Model tab. You can then

choose to apply your choice of configuration to the current viewport (if you want to divide an existing viewport into more viewports, for example) or the entire display (if you want your new configuration to replace the existing configuration).

If you are creating floating viewports on a layout tab, in place of the Apply To drop-down list is the Viewport Spacing box, which enables you to control how much space AutoCAD places between the viewports.

The Setup drop-down list has two choices:

✦ Choose 2D to place the current display in each of the viewports you create, without change.

✦ Choose 3D to create standard orthogonal views (top, right, front) in the viewports — saves you the work of creating them yourself.

If you choose a 3D setup, you can use the Change View To drop-down list to customize which view goes in which viewport. Click any viewport in the Preview pane and choose the view you want for that pane from the drop-down list.

When you've finished setting up your viewports, click OK. If you are creating tiled viewports, AutoCAD automatically creates the viewports according to the configuration you specified. If you are creating floating viewports, AutoCAD prompts you for two points to define a box within which AutoCAD creates the viewports. You can also use the Fit option to create the viewports using the entire printable area of the layout.

Use the Named Viewports tab to restore saved viewport configurations. (You can get to this tab without delay by choosing View⇨Viewports⇨Named Viewports.) Choose the viewport you saved (you can save only tiled viewport configurations) and click OK.

If you are on a layout and already have floating viewports, any viewport configuration you restore or create is added to your existing viewports, usually resulting in viewports on top of viewports. If you want to change the existing configuration, first erase the existing viewport or viewports and then create or restore a new configuration.

Use the Join option on the Viewports submenu to combine two adjacent tiled viewports. Pick the *dominant* viewport first and then pick the secondary one. The new viewport has the zoom, viewpoint, and other features of the dominant one (which simply means that you picked it first).

Choose View⇨Viewports⇨1 Viewport as your panic button for getting rid of all those unruly viewports. You return to one viewport, the default. The one viewport shows the view of the last active viewport.

If you're creating floating viewports, you can use the Polygonal Viewport or Object options on the Viewports submenu to create a polygonal viewport or use an object to shape a viewport. The technique is the same as that described under the MVIEW command.

If you're working in 3D, now is the time to use the DDVPOINT, VPOINT, or 3DORBIT command to do something interesting with your viewports. From paper space, double-click anywhere inside a viewport to make it active, and create different views in each viewport. Even if you're working in 2D, viewports can show different parts of your drawing at different zooms. You can draw from one tiled viewport to another. The possibilities are endless!

More stuff

You can also create floating viewports using the MVIEW command. The MVIEW command offers more control over viewports, letting you turn them on and off, for example.

See Chapter 15 of *AutoCAD 2000 For Dummies*.

WBLOCK

Saves a block as a drawing file on your hard disk. (WBLOCK stands for Write block.)

Command line only

How to use it

AutoCAD opens the Write Block dialog box. Use the Source section to choose what you want to put in the drawing file. If you have already selected a block, the name of the block appears in the text box.

Use the Base Point section to specify a base point for the file. By default, this is 0,0,0. However, if you want to be able to insert the block from a base point on the object, for example, you can choose Pick Point and pick a point on the object. (Use an object snap for accuracy.)

If you haven't already selected your objects or a block (you're not the type that always comes into a dialog box prepared), click Select Objects to return to your drawing and select the objects or block. Press Enter to end object selection and return to the dialog box. Then choose what you want to do with those objects:

✦ Retain keeps them in the drawing.

✦ Convert to block converts individual objects that you selected to a block. The name of the block is the same as the file name you specify in the Destination section.

✦ Delete from drawing makes them go away.

Now use the Destination section of the dialog box to name the drawing file you want to create as well as its location. Use the little button with the ellipsis (. . .) on it to browse to the location. Then choose the units you want the block to use when you drag it into a drawing from the AutoCAD DesignCenter. If you choose Feet, for example, a block two units wide becomes two feet wide when you drag it into a drawing. You can also choose Unitless to avoid scaling. In any event, just for fun, look at the entire list of units — bet there are some that you've never heard of!

See also the BLOCK and INSERT commands for more information.

See Chapter 13 of *AutoCAD 2000 For Dummies* for a discussion on blocks.

WEDGE

Draws a 3D solid wedge.

Toolbar: On the Solids toolbar, click the Wedge button.

Menu: Choose Draw⇨Solids⇨Wedge.

How to use it

At the prompt, specify a first corner for the base of your wedge. Then specify a diagonally opposite base corner. If the Z values of your points are different, AutoCAD uses the difference to create the height of the wedge. If the Z values are the same, AutoCAD prompts you for a height.

The cube option means a wedge with sides of equal length. You still specify the first point. Then right-click, choose Cube, and type a length so that you define the length, width, and height after specifying a first corner.

More stuff

You can enter negative distances to draw the wedge in the direction of the negative axes.

XCLIP

Displays only the portion of an external reference (xref) inside a boundary or plane you specify.

 Toolbar: On the Reference toolbar, click the External Reference Clip button.

Menu: Choose Modify⇨Clip⇨Xref.

How to use it

Select an xref. At the prompt, use the following options:

✦ ON turns on an existing boundary that you had turned off.

✦ OFF turns off an existing boundary so that you can see the entire xref.

✦ Clipdepth creates front and back planes for 3D xrefs. You then see only the part of the xref between the two planes.

✦ Delete deletes an existing boundary.

✦ Generate Polyline creates a polyline on top of an existing clipping boundary. You need to create the clipping boundary first, then reuse XCLIP with this option. You can then use PEDIT to modify the polyline and use the Select Polyline suboption as the new clipping boundary.

✦ New boundary creates a new clipping boundary. (You can press Enter to use this option.) You then have a choice of creating a polygonal or a rectangular boundary. Press Enter to create a rectangular boundary and pick two corners of the rectangle. Right-click and choose Polygonal to create a polygonal boundary and pick all the points you want to create the boundary. Press Enter to complete the boundary. If a clipping boundary already exists, AutoCAD asks whether you want to delete it so you can replace it. You can select an existing polyline to define the new clipping boundary.

When you're finished, AutoCAD displays only the portion of the xref inside the boundary.

More stuff

XCLIP also works on blocks. **See also** the XREF command for more on xrefs.

XLINE

Draws an infinite line (used for construction lines).

Toolbar: On the Draw toolbar, click the Construction Line button.

Menu: Choose Draw⇨Construction Line.

How to use it

AutoCAD prompts for a first point. Because this line theoretically is an infinite line, the point really just defines where the line will be rather than its endpoint. Pick a second through point. AutoCAD creates the xline. No matter how far out you zoom, the line always goes from one end of your screen to the other.

You also can use horizontal and vertical options. You pick one point, and XLINE creates a horizontal or vertical xline. For the Angle option, you specify an angle — either by typing it or referencing a selected object and then typing an angle relative to that object. Then pick a through point.

You can draw an xline that bisects (cuts in half) an angle vertex. Use the Bisect option; then pick an angle vertex, a start point, and an end point.

The Offset option creates an xline parallel to another object. Type an offset distance, select a line, and pick a point that indicates what side to offset. Alternately, use the Through suboption to specify the offset distance by picking a through point.

See also the RAY command.

XPLODE

Breaks blocks and other compound objects into individual components; gives you control over color, layer, and linetype.

Command line only

How to use it

XPLODE prompts you to select objects. If you select more than one explodable object, the next prompt asks you whether you want to explode individually or globally. In either case, the suboptions are the same. If you select individual exploding, AutoCAD highlights objects one at a time so that you can make your decisions individually. Following are the options:

All	Sets the color, linetype, and layer of the individual objects after you explode them. You get the same suboptions as for the Color, LAyer, and Ltype options.
Color	Sets the color of the exploded objects. You can choose any of the standard AutoCAD colors, or you can choose BYBlock or BYLayer. Setting the color to Byblock means that the objects take on the color of the original block.
LAyer	Sets the layer of the exploded objects; otherwise, they take on the current layer.
LType	Sets the linetype of the exploded objects. You can choose BYBlock, BYLayer, CONTinuous, or other loaded linetypes. Setting the linetype to Byblock means that the objects take on the linetype of the original block.
Inherit from parent block	In AutoCAD language, it means that the color, linetype, and layer of the exploded objects are the same as the exploded block if its layer is 0 and the linetype is BYBLOCK.
Explode	Same as the EXPLODE command.

XREF & XATTACH

Manages references to external files. (In AutoSpeak, *xref* stands *for external reference.*)

 Toolbar: On the Reference toolbar, click the External Reference button.

Menu: Choose Insert⇨Xref Manager.

How to use it

Xrefs are external drawings that you insert into your drawing. You use xrefs in much the same way that you use blocks. The main value of xrefs is that each time you open or plot your drawing, the xrefs are reloaded, so any changes in the external drawings are reflected in your drawing. Also, the actual external drawing is not a part of your drawing — your drawing only contains a reference to the other drawing, keeping drawing size smaller.

The Xref Manager dialog box lists your xrefs in a plain list, if the List View button is depressed. If the Tree View button is depressed, your xrefs are listed in hierarchical format so that you can see whether any xrefs are nested inside other xrefs.

To attach an xref, click Attach. In the Select File to Attach dialog box, choose a file and click Open. (The XATTACH command opens the Select File to Attach dialog box without any intermediate steps.) The External Reference dialog box opens where you can specify the insertion point, scale and rotation or choose to specify them on-screen. Click OK.

In the Xref Manager, you can choose any listed xref and use the buttons to do the following:

Detach	Erases the xref and deletes the reference to the external drawing. The advantage of using this option instead of simply erasing the xref is that you also get rid of the layers, colors, linetypes, and other elements of the xref.
Reload	If someone else changes the external drawing while you're working in your drawing, enables you to reload the xref to see the changes. (Wait until that person has finished making the changes!)
Unload	Removes the xref's display. The reference, however, is still available so that you can reload it at any time.
Bind	Turns an xref into a block. You have two choices: binding, which keeps the xref's layer names in a format that makes where the layer came from clear, and inserting, which strips out the source information.

The bottom of the dialog box displays the location where AutoCAD found the xref. If someone (not you, of course) had the nerve to rename or move the external drawing that you're referencing, your drawing won't be able to find it. Click Browse to find the xref. Click Save Path to save the new name and path.

More stuff

See Chapter 13 of *AutoCAD 2000 For Dummies*.

ZOOM

Magnifies or shrinks the display of objects in your drawing.

Toolbar: On the Standard toolbar, use the Zoom flyout.

Menu: Choose View⇨Zoom.

How to use it

Real-time Zoom enables you to zoom in and out as you move the cursor. Choose Zoom Realtime from the Standard toolbar. Move the magnifying glass cursor up to zoom in and down to zoom out. Press Esc or Enter to exit real-time zoom mode — or start another command using a menu or toolbar. Right-click to open a menu that enables you to switch to pan mode, exit, or use other ZOOM options.

If you have an IntelliMouse (a mouse with a wheel on it), you can zoom using the wheel. Roll the wheel down to zoom out; up to zoom in.

AutoCAD offers lots of zooming options. Each option has a separate icon on the Zoom flyout:

Zoom Previous	Displays the preceding view. You can use this option up to 10 times before AutoCAD forgets.
Zoom Window	Enables you to pick two opposite corners of the display that you want to see.
Zoom Dynamic	Enables you to pan and zoom at the same time. The display zooms out, and a view box appears. This view box alternates between pan and zoom mode. The box starts out as a pan box, indicated by an *X* in the middle. Drag the box until you find the location you want in the drawing; then click that location. You switch to zoom mode, which is indicated by an arrow at one edge. Move your mouse, and you see that the view box changes size instead of moving around the drawing. Resize the box until you have the window you want to see. Press Enter to complete the command, or click to return to pan mode.
Zoom Scale (X/XP)	Typing a number scales the display relative to the drawing limits. If you type **3**, the display appears three times the size you'd see after using Zoom with the All option. This option can be confusing if you have another zoom value. So you can type **3x**, which scales the display relative to your current view. If you type **3xp**, AutoCAD scales the display relative to paper space units; use this format when in paper space.
Zoom Center	Enables you to pick a center point for the new view, and then specify a magnification or height. A height is a plain number that represents drawing units. Type **10**, for example, to get a display that's 10 drawing units high. To specify magnification, type a number followed by x — for example, **10x**, which magnifies the display by 10.
Zoom In	Equivalent to using Zoom Scale 2x — that is, it doubles the size of the display.
Zoom Out	Equivalent to using Zoom Scale .5x — that is, it halves the size of the display.
Zoom All	Zooms to the drawing limits or extents, whichever is greater. If you're using a 3D view, this option is equivalent to using Zoom Extents.
Zoom Extents	Displays the entire extents of the drawing.

The System Variables

In this part of the book, you enter the exotic, arcane world of system variables. *System variables* are simply values that AutoCAD stores for all sorts of settings. These variables enable you to fine-tune the way that AutoCAD works. Many system variables just provide information and, to tell you the truth, a lot of them are used only in AutoLISP programs.

In this part . . .

✔ **Fine-tuning the way AutoCAD works**

✔ **Using system variables to get information**

Using System Variables

Once upon a time, you had to use system variables a lot. Nowadays, many variables are handled automatically by the choices that you make in dialog boxes. When you use the DIMSTYLE command to create a dimension style, for example, you're working with system variables without knowing it (which is the best way, believe me).

I've included here some system variables that aren't accessible by regular commands, as well as a few other variables that are more convenient to use on the command line. You may want to use these variables directly. I left out some additional system variables that apply only to customizing AutoCAD or using AutoLISP program routines. I categorized the system variables by type to help you find them more easily.

Type the name of the system variable on the command line and press Enter. Then, if applicable, type its value and press Enter. If the system variable just provides information, you don't type a value.

Many system variables only turn things on and off. A value of 0 means off; a value of 1 means on — usually!

To see the options available for a system variable, type the system variable name, press Enter, and press F1.

I hope this list can speed you on your way. Most lists of system variables are not useful, but on the rare occasions when you need to use a system variable, look here. (For more information, choose Help⇨AutoCAD Help Topics. From the Contents tab, double-click Command Reference and then double-click System Variables.)

3D

DISPSILH. Related to the ISOLINES system variable, which sets the number of lines on a 3D surface. DISPSILH turns on (1) and off (0) the display of silhouette curves of solid objects in wire-frame mode, so that no matter which viewpoint you use, you always see an isoline showing you the shape of the curve.

FACETRES. Affects the smoothness of 3D objects that are shaded or have hidden lines. You can set this variable from .01 to 10.

HIDEPRECISION. Controls the precision of calculations for hides and shades. The default, 0, uses normal precision. Set it to 1 to specify double precision to calculate the hide. A setting of 1 requires more memory than a setting of 0.

ISOLINES. The number of isolines per surface on an object; this number can range from 0 to 2047. The default is 4, which is puny. Do a regen after using this to see the result.

SHADEDGE. Controls the way edges are shaded. Values are

0	Shades faces, but edges are not highlighted
1	Shades faces and highlights edges with the background color
2	Doesn't shade faces, hides hidden lines, shows edges using the object color
3	Highlights edges using only the background color

Even though 1 is probably the most useful setting, 3 is the default.

SHADEDIF. Sets the percent of diffuse reflective light to ambient light. The default is 70. You might find 50 to be a useful value. Values can range from 0 to 100.

SURFTAB1. The number of tabulations used in the RULESURF and TABSURF commands. Also, for the REVSURF and EDGESURF commands, this variable sets the M (row) direction.

SURFTAB2. Sets the N (column) direction for the REVSURF and EDGESURF commands.

SURFU. The surface density in the M (row) direction. Applies to polyface meshes, such as the meshes created by 3DMESH.

SURFV. The surface density in the N (column) direction. Applies to polyface meshes, such as the meshes created by 3DMESH.

UCSFOLLOW. Determines whether AutoCAD returns you to plan view when you change the UCS. A value of 0 (the default) means you don't return to plan view; 1 means you do.

 UCSORTHO. Sets whether the related UCS is automatically restored when you change to an orthographic view such as Top, Bottom, or Left. This is on by default, a new style of functioning for AutoCAD, just to drive you bananas.

Attributes

ATTDIA. Determines whether you get a dialog box when you use the INSERT command to insert a block that contains attributes. A setting of 0 says you don't get the dialog box; a setting of 1 says you do.

ATTREQ. With a setting of 0, AutoCAD uses default attribute values when you insert a block with attributes. With a setting of 1 (the default), AutoCAD prompts you for values.

Dimensioning

DIMASO. Turns associative dimensioning on and off. If associative dimensioning is off, the parts of the dimension are separate objects and don't adjust when you change the dimensioned objects. The variable's values are ON and OFF.

DIMSHO. When this variable is on, associative dimensions are recomputed continually as you drag an object. (Associative dimensions change automatically when you change the object.) If this feature slows your computer, turn DIMSHO off.

Drawing Aids

BLIPMODE. Turns blips on and off.

EXPERT. This variable is for the experts among you who get annoyed when AutoCAD asks things such as Block already defined. Redefine it? ("Of course, I want to redefine it; why do you think I'm doing this?") A value of 0 is the normal setting. Values ranging from 1 to 5 suppress more and more prompts.

MAXACTVP. Specifies the maximum number of viewports regenerated at one time. The default is 64.

MBUTTONPAN. Lets you use the third button or wheel on your mouse or digitizing puck to pan, overriding the menu definition.

PICKSTYLE. Determines the way groups and hatches can be selected.

0	No group selection. Hatches are selected without their boundaries.
1	Group selection. Hatches are selected without their boundaries.
2	No group selection. Hatches are selected along with their boundaries.
3	Group selection. Hatches are selected along with their boundaries.

UCSBASE. Stores the name of a UCS that defines the origin and orientation of orthographic UCS settings. You can use any named UCS.

UNITMODE. Determines how fractional, feet-and-inches, and surveyor's angle units are displayed on the status line. Set it to 1 to display them in input format, as in 3'2-1/2". A value of 0, the default, displays the same number as 3'-2 1/2".

VISRETAIN. Sets the visibility of layers in xref files. A setting of 0 means xrefs take on the layer definition in the current drawing. A setting of 1 means the layer settings in the xref drawing take precedence.

WHIPARC. Sets whether arcs and circles are displayed as a series of vectors (the default) or as true, smooth curves.

WORLDVIEW. Determines whether the UCS changes to the WCS when you use DVIEW, 3DORBIT, or VPOINT. A value of 0 means the UCS remains unchanged; a value of 1 means it switches to the WCS; and a value of 2 means the UCS changes to the UCS you specified in the UCSBASE system variable.

 ZOOMFACTOR. Controls the incremental change in zoom created by one push or pull of the Intellimouse wheel.

Edits

DELOBJ. Determines whether objects used to create other objects are maintained in the drawing database. The default (1) retains these objects; a value of 0 deletes them.

EXPLMODE. Determines whether EXPLODE explodes blocks that are nonuniformly scaled (NUS), which means the X and Y scales are different. The default (1) is to explode them, but you can turn the feature off (0).

MIRRTEXT. When you're mirroring objects that include text, a value of 1 (the default) mirrors the text just like anything else. A value of 0 keeps the text looking normal, so that you don't need to look in a mirror to read it. This variable is a good one to know.

WMFBKGND. Lets you control the background of Windows metafile objects, whether created using WMFOUT, copied to the clipboard and pasted as a metafile, or dragged and dropped as a metafile. You can set the background to transparent or have it take on the background color of your drawing screen (the default). This variable is useful when you paste WMF files into other programs with unusual background colors.

Information/Customization

Most of the variables in this section only provide information. Many of the variables are *read-only,* which means you can look at them and sigh, but you can't change anything.

ACADPREFIX. The directory path of the ACAD environment.

ACADVER. The AutoCAD version number.

AREA. The last area calculated by AREA, LIST, or DBLIST, in case you forgot.

AUDITCTL. Turn this variable on (a value of 1) to create an audit report file.

CDATE. Sets the date and time.

CMDACTIVE. Stores what kind of command is active.

CMDDIA. Turns dialog boxes on and off. If you set this variable to 0, you won't see dialog boxes. The default is 1.

CMDNAMES. The name of the active command.

DATE. The date and time in Julian format.

DCTCUST. The custom spelling dictionary file.

DCTMAIN. The main spelling dictionary file.

DISTANCE. The last distance calculated by the DIST command, in case you forgot.

DWGNAME. The drawing name.

DWGPREFIX. The path for the drawing.

DWGTITLED. Indicates whether you've named your drawing.

EXTMAX. The upper-right corner of the drawing extents.

EXTMIN. The lower-left corner of the drawing extents.

FILEDIA. Turns on (1) and off (0) the display of dialog boxes that deal with files, such as the Open dialog box.

INSNAME. Stores a default block name for the INSERT command.

LASTANGLE. The end angle of the last arc you drew.

LASTPOINT. The last point entered.

LASTPROMPT. Stores the last text string that appears on the command line, including your input.

LIMMAX. The upper-right drawing limits.

LIMMIN. The lower-left drawing limits.

LOCALE. The ISO (International Standards Organization) language code of the current AutoCAD version.

LOGINNAME. The user's name (probably you). This is for networks that require a log on name.

MENUECHO. Sets menu echo and display prompting.

MENUNAME. The current menu name.

OLEHIDE. Specifies whether OLE objects (objects you embed or link into your drawing) are visible and printed, and if so, where. The default (0) makes them visible everywhere. 1 makes them visible only on a layout tab. 2 makes them visible only on the Model tab. 3 hides them everywhere.

PERIMETER. The last perimeter value calculated by AREA, LIST, or DBLIST, in case you forgot.

PFACEVMAX. The maximum number of vertices per face.

PLATFORM. The computer platform you're using (Windows or Windows NT, stage right, stage left, and so on).

RASTERPREVIEW. Determines whether drawing preview images are saved with the drawing and what type of images are saved. By default, AutoCAD saves previews.

SAVEFILE. Stores the filename that AutoCAD uses in autosaving. Set the autosave time by choosing Tools⇨Options⇨Open and Save tab.

SAVENAME. Stores the filename to which you saved the drawing.

SCREENSIZE. The size, in pixels, of the current viewport.

SHPNAME. The default shape name.

TDCREATE. The date and time the drawing was created.

TEMPPREFIX. Sets a folder name for temporary files.

VIEWCTR. The center of the view of the current viewport.

WORLDUCS. Stores whether the UCS is the same as the world coordinate system. A value of 0 means the UCS is different; a value of 1 means the UCS and WCS are the same.

XREFCTL. Set to 1 to create an xref log file. Set to 0 if you don't want to create a log file.

Object Creation

2000

CELWEIGHT. Sets the current line weight for new objects.

INSNAME. Stores a default block name for INSERT.

PELLIPSE. Determines whether the ELLIPSE command creates a true ellipse (0, the default) or a polyline representation of an ellipse (1). The concept of a polyline ellipse is a holdover from previous releases of AutoCAD.

PLINEGEN. When set to 0, the default, line types start each vertex of a polyline with a dash. When set to 1, the line type is generated in a continuous pattern regardless of the vertices.

PLINETYPE. The value controls the conversion and creation of lightweight polylines, the type used since Release 14. At 0, polylines in previous release drawings aren't converted when opened in AutoCAD 2000 and AutoCAD creates the old-format polylines. At 1, polylines in previous release drawings aren't converted when opened in AutoCAD 2000 and AutoCAD creates lightweight polylines. At 2 (the default), polylines in previous release drawings are converted when opened in AutoCAD 2000 and AutoCAD creates lightweight polylines. This system variable affects all commands that create polylines, for example PLINE, RECTANG, and POLYGON.

POLYSIDES. The default number of sides for a polygon.

SKPOLY. A value of 0 means SKETCH creates lines; a value of 1 means it creates polylines.

SPLFRAME. Sets the spline-fit polyline display. If the value is 0, the frame that controls a spline or polygon mesh isn't displayed; also, invisible edges of 3D faces and polyface meshes aren't displayed. If the value is 1, you see the frame of a spline or polygon mesh and invisible edges of 3D faces and polyface meshes.

SPLINESEGS. Sets the number of line segments that each spline generates. A higher number results in a curve that more precisely matches the frame.

SPLINETYPE. Determines the type of spline curve created by PEDIT spline. Use 5 for quadratic B-spline or 6 for cubic B-spline.

SURFTYPE. Sets the type of surface fitting used by the PEDIT Smooth option for 3D Polygon Meshes. Use 5 for a quadratic B-spline, 6 for a cubic B-spline, and 8 for a Bezier surface.

Text

FONTALT. Sets an alternative font that AutoCAD uses, if the font you ask for can't be found. (Little AutoCAD lost her fonts and didn't know where to find them.)

TEXTQLTY. Sets the resolution of TrueType fonts. Values represent dots per inch. Now this variable affects only rendering, printer output, plotter output, and exporting with PSOUT.

TEXTSIZE. Stores the default or last height for text styles without a fixed height.

TEXTSTYLE. The current text-style name.

Part IV

The Toolbars

This part guides you through the toolbars. If you want to do something in AutoCAD but don't know the command name, try looking here. Toolbars are usually organized by function; you can skim through the possibilities and find the command you need.

In this part . . .

✔ Using toolbars

✔ Finding buttons on toolbars and flyouts

Using the Toolbars

The toolbar tooltips are not always the same as the command name. The tooltips sometimes make more sense, whereas the command names are often unintelligible abbreviations. Luckily, when you pass the cursor over a toolbar button, the command name and a brief description usually appear on the status bar. If not, here's another way to find the name of the command:

1. Click a toolbar button that looks useful.

2. At the next prompt, press Esc to cancel the command.

3. Look on the command line. You should see the name of the command. If the command name scrolls by too fast for you to see, press F2 to open the text screen. (Press F2 again to return to your drawing.)

4. Look up the command in Part II.

Here's a warning about tooltips which give you some tip about the function of the button. Sometimes a tip such as the one AutoCAD gives you can be your worst enemy. The most you can say is that it's sometimes like a foul tip when the batter has two strikes: It keeps you in the game but doesn't get you anywhere. And those little pictures don't always do a good job of communicating the button's function either — sometimes, a word is worth a thousand pictures. This part includes the tooltip name next to each button. Don't forget to look on the status bar when the tooltip pops up for the short explanation that appears — it may provide the information you need.

Some toolbars have flyouts. You can tell which ones they are by the little black arrow at the bottom of the button. The flyouts are also available as toolbars. For buttons that have flyouts, I indicate the flyout name. You can then find the buttons listed under the toolbar of the same name. For example, the Standard toolbar contains a button called Named Views. This is just the first button on the View flyout. Look up the Viewpoint toolbar to see all the buttons. By the way, by default, if you click another button on a flyout — not the first one — the one you clicked moves to the top. This can get frustrating — for example, you can't find the Named Views button on the Standard toolbar if you've recently clicked one of the buttons on the View flyout. To find it, click and hold the mouse button where the button used to be — you remember where that was, don't you? — and you can then find it on the flyout.

AutoCAD Toolbars

The Standard toolbar

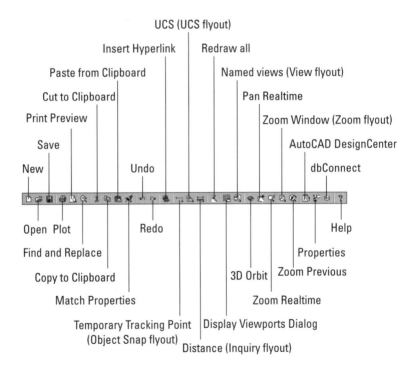

The Object Snap flyout/toolbar

Temporary Tracking Point

Snap to Endpoint

Snap to Intersection

Snap to Extension

Snap to Quadrant

Snap to Perpendicular

Snap to Insert

Snap to Nearest

Object Snap Settings

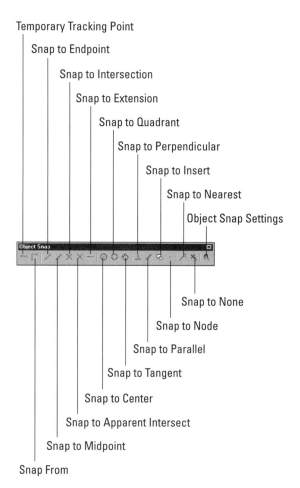

Snap to None

Snap to Node

Snap to Parallel

Snap to Tangent

Snap to Center

Snap to Apparent Intersect

Snap to Midpoint

Snap From

The UCS flyout/toolbar

UCS Previous

Object UCS

View UCS

Z Axis Vector UCS

X Axis Rotate UCS

UCS

Z Axis Rotate UCS

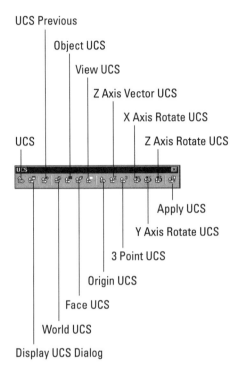

Apply UCS

Y Axis Rotate UCS

3 Point UCS

Origin UCS

Face UCS

World UCS

Display UCS Dialog

The Inquiry flyout/toolbar

Distance

Area

Locate Point

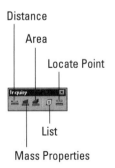

List

Mass Properties

The View flyout/toolbar

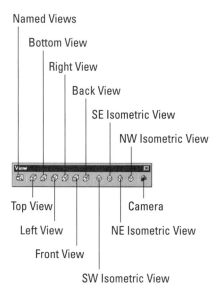

Named Views
Bottom View
Right View
Back View
SE Isometric View
NW Isometric View

Top View
Left View
Front View
SW Isometric View

Camera
NE Isometric View

The Zoom flyout/toolbar

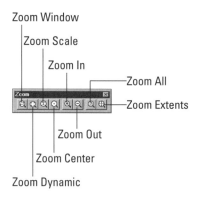

Zoom Window
Zoom Scale
Zoom In
Zoom All
Zoom Extents

Zoom Out
Zoom Center
Zoom Dynamic

The Object Properties toolbar

Make Object's Layer Current   Linetype Control

     Layer Control   Plot Style Control

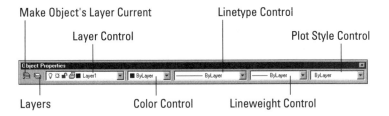

Layers   Color Control   Lineweight Control

The Draw toolbar

     Polygon   Insert Block (Insert flyout)

Multiline   Spline   Point

Line   Arc   Region

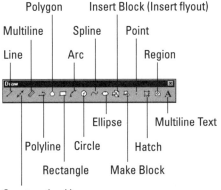

     Ellipse   Multiline Text

Polyline   Circle   Hatch

     Rectangle   Make Block

Construction Line

The Insert flyout/toolbar

Insert Block

     Image

         OLE Object

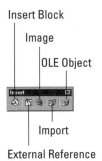

       Import

External Reference

The Modify toolbar

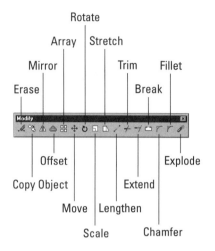

Rotate

Array | Stretch

Mirror | Trim | Fillet

Erase | Break

Offset | Explode

Copy Object | Extend

Move | Lengthen

Scale | Chamfer

The 3D Orbit toolbar

3D Pan

3D Orbit

3D Swivel

3D Adjust Clip Planes

Back Clip On/Off

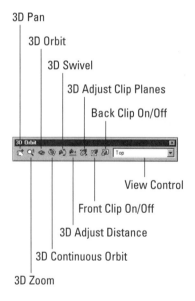

View Control

Front Clip On/Off

3D Adjust Distance

3D Continuous Orbit

3D Zoom

The Dimension toolbar

Linear Dimension
Ordinate Dimension
Diameter Dimension
Quick Dimension
Continue Dimension
Tolerance
Dimension Edit
Dimension Update
Dimension Style

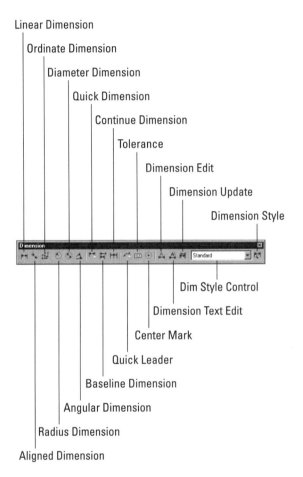

Dim Style Control
Dimension Text Edit
Center Mark
Quick Leader
Baseline Dimension
Angular Dimension
Radius Dimension
Aligned Dimension

The Layouts toolbar

New Layout
Page Setup

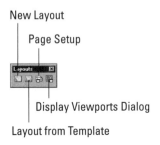

Display Viewports Dialog
Layout from Template

The Modify II toolbar

Draw Order

  Edit Polyline

    Edit Multiline

      Edit Text

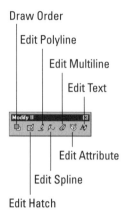

    Edit Attribute

  Edit Spline

Edit Hatch

The Refedit toolbar

Edit block or Xref

  Add objects to working set

    Discard changes to reference

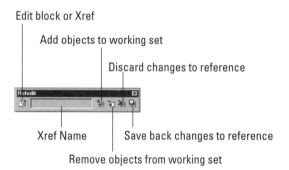

  Xref Name   Save back changes to reference

    Remove objects from working set

The Reference toolbar

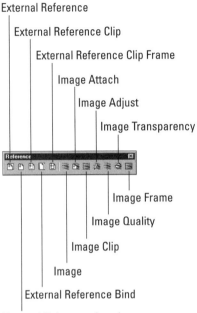

External Reference
External Reference Clip
External Reference Clip Frame
Image Attach
Image Adjust
Image Transparency

Image Frame
Image Quality
Image Clip
Image
External Reference Bind
External Reference Attach

The Render toolbar

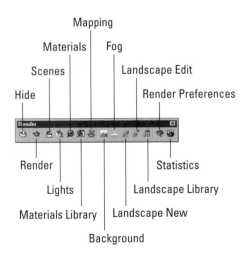

Mapping
Materials
Scenes
Hide
Fog
Landscape Edit
Render Preferences

Render
Lights
Materials Library
Statistics
Landscape Library
Landscape New
Background

The Shade toolbar

2D Wireframe

Gouraud Shaded

Hidden | Gouraud Shaded, Edges On

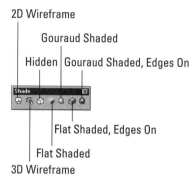

Flat Shaded, Edges On

Flat Shaded

3D Wireframe

The Solids toolbar

Extrude

Wedge | Slice

Cylinder | Interfere

Box | Setup view

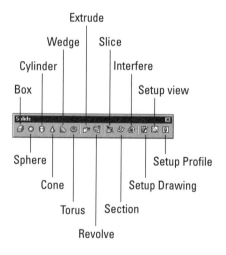

Sphere | Setup Profile

Cone | Setup Drawing

Torus | Section

Revolve

The Solids Editing toolbar

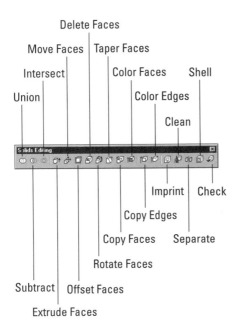

The Surfaces toolbar

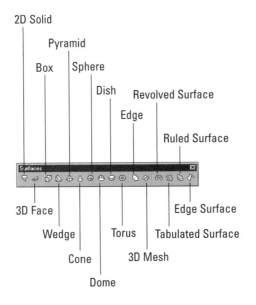

The UCS II toolbar

Display UCS Dialog

Preset and Orthographic

Move UCS Origin

The Viewports toolbar

Display Viewports Dialog

Polygonal Viewport

Clip Existing Viewport

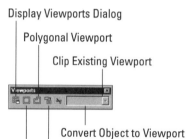

Convert Object to Viewport

Viewport Scale Control

Single Viewport

The Web toolbar

Go Back

Stop Navigation

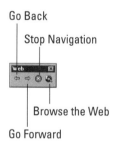

Browse the Web

Go Forward

Techie Talk

acquire a point. During object snap tracking, you pass the cursor over an object snap to acquire it. Then move the cursor to the general area of the new point you want to find. AutoCAD places tracking lines from the acquired points so you can visually see the relationships between the acquired points and your new point. When you pass the cursor over an acquired point, it becomes unacquired (no need to feel sorry for it) and the cross disappears.

alias. A short name for an AutoCAD command. You can customize the ACAD.PGP file to create your own — for example, CI for CIRCLE and CO for COPY.

ambient light. The overall background light used for rendering.

annotation. Text, dimensions, tolerances, symbols, or notes that explain a drawing.

aperture. The little box that appears when you use an object snap. The aperture is different from the pickbox.

associative. Applies to dimensions and hatches; the term means that these elements adjust themselves when you change the objects to which they're attached.

attribute. Text attached to a block that can be assigned a specific value each time the block is inserted. All these values can be extracted and turned into a database, such as a bill of materials.

AutoCAD Design Center (ADC). AutoCAD 2000's new feature that lets you drag layers, layouts, blocks, and other drawings into your drawing.

AutoLISP. The AutoCAD version of the LISP programming language. You can use AutoLISP to write programs that control the way AutoCAD functions.

AutoSnap. AutoCAD's way of letting you know when you're in the neighborhood of an object snap. You see a Snap Tip with the object snap's type (Endpoint, Midpoint, or such) as well as a marker — a shape that indicates the object snap's location. You also feel a slight pull of the cursor toward the object snap.

AutoTracking. AutoCAD's method for letting you locate new points based on existing object snaps (object snap tracking) or falling along certain angles (polar tracking).

B-spline. A curve defined by points you choose; also called a *NURBS curve.*

bind. To turn an external reference (xref) into a regular block.

bitmap. A type of graphic defined by pixel or dots (rather than by vectors).

blips. Little markers on the screen that show where you specified a point. REDRAW gets rid of blips.

block. One or more objects grouped so that they function as a single object.

Boolean operation. Adding, subtracting, or intersecting solids or 2D regions.

boundary. A closed region or polyline.

BYBLOCK. The object takes its the color or line type from any block containing it.

BYLAYER. The object takes its color and line type from its layer definition; you don't set the color and line type.

Cartesian coordinate system. A way of defining point locations using three perpendicular X, Y, Z axes.

chord. A line that connects two points on a circle or arc.

clipping planes. Planes that cut off the field of view.

clipping viewports. A feature enabling you to view only the portion of a viewport within a border.

continuous orbit. The cool way to get dizzy. In 3DORBIT, a continuous orbit lets you start the direction of a motion and let go. 3DORBIT continues to turn your model in the same direction until you stop it by choosing Orbit from the shortcut menu.

control point. A point (usually, many points) that AutoCAD creates to define a spline.

cycling. A way of going through all the object snap points within the aperture box. Press Tab until you get the object snap you want.

digitizer. An electronic flat board that enables you to draw and execute commands with the tablet template. You usually use something called a puck, which is similar to a mouse but has crosshairs that provide exact point specification.

DWF. Drawing Web File. A format for a file that you can place on a Web site. The viewer of the file can pan, zoom, and print, but can't access the actual drawing objects.

DXF. Drawing Interchange Format. An ASCII file format that contains all the information of a drawing. DXF is used to import or export drawings between programs.

entity. Another word for an object (anything in your drawing).

ePlot. Stands for electronic plot. A new expression for creating DWF files. You create these files using the PLOT command.

explode. To break a block into its original objects.

external reference (xref). Another file that's referenced in your file, creating a link between the two.

fence. A set of lines that you use to select objects. Anything that crosses the fence gets sent to jail for trespassing.

fit points. Points you specify when defining a spline.

floating viewports. Bordered views of a drawing that show different viewpoints or zooms of your objects. Floating viewports, which are created on any layout tab, are objects that you can move, resize, and delete.

flyout. A bunch of hidden buttons that fly out when you click a button on a toolbar. A flyout is equivalent to a secondary menu.

freeze. A mode for a layer that means the layer isn't displayed, regenerated, or plotted.

Gouraud shading. A type of shading of 3D objects that provides gradual shading from face to face, providing a more realistic look than flat shading.

grid. A rectangular grid of regularly spaced dots that cover the screen. Grids help you get a feel for the unit size and assist you in drawing; if you don't like them, just grid and bear it.

grips. Small squares that appear on objects when you select them. You can use grips to modify the objects directly.

group. A named group of objects that you can select and modify as a group.

hatch. A pattern of lines (or a solid fill) used to fill a closed area to indicate shading or a type of material (bricks, grass, and so on).

hidden surfaces. Surfaces that would be hidden from a certain viewpoint. These surfaces are hidden when using HIDE, SHADE, or RENDER.

image tile. A type of menu that shows your options as small images. You can click an image to choose an option.

imprinting. A way to place the outline of an object on a solid.

in-place reference editing. Editing of an external reference (or a block) from within the current drawing.

island. An enclosed area in a hatch area — for example, a small circle in a big circle.

isolines. Lines that AutoCAD uses to show the curve of a surface. Isolines are similar to tessellation lines.

isometric drawing. A drawing that places the X,Y,Z axes 120 degrees from one another and is used in 2D drawing to give the appearance of 3D objects.

layout. What AutoCAD used to call paper space. A layout is for laying out a drawing on an imaginary sheet of paper. You click a layout tab to get to a layout.

linetype. A type of line. The linetype indicates whether the line is continuous or formed of dots, dashes, and spaces.

lineweight. The width of a line. You can assign a lineweight to a layer. Click the LWT button on the status bar to display your objects' lineweights on the screen.

M direction. When AutoCAD draws 3D meshes, the M direction is set by the way you define the first and second rows. But because you're in 3D, a row can face any direction.

M size. When AutoCAD draws polygon meshes, the M size is the number of rows.

mass properties. Properties of an object that has volume, such as its center of gravity.

materials. Materials are used in rendering. Materials are called by the names of real materials — such as steel, glass, and plastic — and are defined by their color, reflective qualities, roughness (which affects highlights created by a light source), transparency, and so on. Materials are attached to objects.

MDI/MDE. Multiple Document Interface/Environment. Enables you to open as many drawings as your computer's memory allows. You can easily copy and paste objects from one open drawing to another.

mesh. A bunch of connected polygons that create faces and that together represent the surface of a curved object. By specifying the vertices of the polygons, you define the surface. A mesh has no mass or weight properties (unlike solids) but can be shaded and rendered.

model. A 2D or 3D drawing of a real object. AutoCAD has three 3D-model types: wire frame, surface, and solid.

model space. The place where you create models, which means where you draw. You get to model space by clicking the Model tab on the drawing area. Model space is different from paper space (a layout), in which you can lay out your drawing for plotting (if you want).

node. The same as a point. You use the Node object snap to locate a point object.

normal. A line that's perpendicular to a plane or a surface; it's used to define a new plane in some editing commands.

Noun/Verb Selection. Selecting the object (noun) before the command (verb). You turn this feature on or off on the Selection tab of the Options dialog box.

NURBS. Nonuniform rational B-spline. A B-spline defined by a series of points.

object. Anything that's considered to be one element in your drawing, such as a line, a circle, or a line of text. An object is the same as an entity.

Object Property Manager (OPM). Also known as the Property window. You can change the properties of objects from this window. New for AutoCAD 2000.

object snap. Called OSNAP in AutoSpeak. Geometric points on an object that you can select automatically — for example, endpoints, midpoints, and circle centers.

ortho mode. A setting that limits you to drawing horizontally or vertically.

orthogonal. Having perpendicular intersections.

OSNAP. *See* object snap.

paper space. A drawing mode used for laying out a drawing for plotting. Also called a layout. In paper space, you create floating viewports with different views of your drawing.

parallel projection. A way of viewing a 3D object without showing perspective.

partial open/partial load. In AutoCAD 2000, you can partially open a drawing or partially load additional elements in a partially opened drawing. You use the Open dialog box and choose the layers and views that you want to open and display.

pickbox. The little box that appears at the cursor when you see a `Select objects` prompt. You can change the size of the pickbox by using the Selection tab of the Options dialog box.

pixel. Short for picture element. Pixels are the teensy-weensy dots that make up the picture on your screen. Certain graphics programs enable you to change graphics pixel by pixel.

plan view. The view of an object looking straight down from above. Plan view is the only accurate view for 2D objects but only one possible view for 3D objects.

plot style. A collection of settings that determines how an object is plotted. A plot style is an object property. A plot style includes settings for color, dithering, grayscale, screening, line type, line end and join style, and fill style, among others.

plot style table. A file that contains a collection of plot styles. Two types of plot style tables are available — color dependent and named.

point filters. A way of extracting a coordinate point by filtering out one or two of the X, Y, or Z coordinates.

polar snap. A kind of snap. (The other kind is a grid snap.) Enables you to snap to specified increments along an angle, such as every .5 units along a 45-degree angle.

polyline. A group of lines and arcs that are treated as one object.

primitive. A basic 3D shape, such as a box, a wedge, a cone, a cylinder, a sphere, or a torus.

puck. A tool for drawing and choosing menu or toolbar commands when you have a digitizer. It looks somewhat like a mouse but has a transparent area with crosshairs for precise picking of points.

raster image. An image or graphics created by converting math or digital information into a series of dots.

real-time pan and zoom. A way of panning and zooming in which the display changes as you move the mouse cursor.

redraw. To refresh the screen, thereby getting rid of blip marks and stray remains of editing commands.

region. A closed 2D area that functions like a 2D surface.

right-hand rule. A hokey but effective way to figure out which way is up (which way the Z axis goes). Hold the back of your right hand near the screen. Point your thumb in the direction of the positive X axis. Point your index finger up in the direction of the positive Y axis. Stick your other fingers straight out at right angles to your index finger. That's the direction of the positive Z axis. The direction of the curve of your other fingers also indicates the direction of positive rotation.

roughness. The spread of the highlight produced by a material's reflection.

ruled surface. A surface created between two curves or between a point and a curve.

running object snap. An object snap that stays on until you turn it off. If you have a running endpoint object snap, every time you select an object, you're selecting the endpoint of the object. It's also a warning that if you run into an object, something might go snap.

selection set. The group of objects you've selected.

shape. A special kind of object defined with certain customization codes and compiled into a compressed form. Shape usually refers to fonts or shapes placed in line types; it doesn't mean any old regular shape that you draw on your screen.

shelling. A way to hollow out a 3D solid so that it has walls around its perimeter.

snap. When snap is on, the cursor jumps to the nearest point defined by the snap spacing; you can't get to anything in between. The two types of snap are grid and polar.

spline. A smooth curve passing through or near points that you specify. AutoCAD uses a particular kind of spline called a NURBS curve. (Sounds nurby to me.)

stacked fraction. A fraction in which the numerator is on top of the denominator, usually with a horizontal line between them (so they don't get tangled in each other).

support file search path. Where AutoCAD looks for supporting files containing fonts, drawings to insert, menus, line types, and hatch patterns. You can add any folder on your hard drive to the support file search path using the Files tab of the Options dialog box.

surface. A topological 2D area. You can create a surface by using surface commands, such as 3D, 3DMESH, TABSURF, RULESURF, and REVSURF.

system variable. Variables storing modes and values that affect the way AutoCAD functions. Some system variables are read-only; many others, you can set.

tabulated surface. A kind of ruled surface defined by a curve and a line or a polyline that indicates a direction.

template. A file that contains certain settings (layers, styles, and so on) and is used as the basis for new drawings.

temporary files. AutoCAD creates temporary files during a drawing session. These files are usually closed when you exit, but if your system crashes, they might be left on your hard disk.

tessellation lines. Lines that help you visualize a curved, 3D surface.

tiled model space. A drawing mode in which you can divide the drawing space into viewports that can't be overlapped and that are arranged next to one another like floor tiles. You must be on the Model tab.

tolerances. The amount of variance allowed in an object. Tolerances appear after a dimension and can be shown as limits tolerances or plus/minus tolerances.

tooltip. The description of a button when you put the cursor over a toolbar button for a few seconds. Tooltips are supposed to be helpful.

Tracking. A substitute for point filters that enables you to locate a point based on the coordinates of existing objects. You can use object snap tracking or polar tracking.

transparent commands. Commands that can be used while you're in the middle of another command. When you type them on the command line, type an apostrophe (') before the command name. Most commands that don't change the view can be used transparently.

unit. Any distance that you use for measuring. The unit is the basis of all coordinates. When you plot your drawing, you can set the unit equal to inches or millimeters.

user coordinate system. A coordinate system you define by specifying where the origin is (relative to the world coordinate system), as well as the direction of the X, Y, Z axes.

vector. Any object that has direction and length, such as a line.

viewpoint. A location in 3D from which you can view your drawing.

viewport. A border that displays all or part of your drawing inside it. The two types of viewports are tiled and floating. You use tiled viewports on the Model tab. You use floating viewports on a layout tab; these viewports are actual objects that you can edit.

WHIP! A program that enables you to view DWF files. WHIP! is included with AutoCAD 2000.

wire frame. A representation of a 3D object made using lines and arcs. Also, the display of surfaces and solids that looks like it's made out of lines and arcs.

world coordinate system. A coordinate system used as the basis for all other systems you may define.

Index

D

E

YOUR ONLINE RESOURCE

WWW.DUMMIES.COM

Discover *Dummies*™ Online!

The *Dummies* Web Site is your fun and friendly online resource for the latest information about *...For Dummies*® books on all your favorite topics. From cars to computers, wine to Windows, and investing to the Internet, we've got a shelf full of *...For Dummies* books waiting for you!

Ten Fun and Useful Things You Can Do at www.dummies.com

1. Register this book and win!
2. Find and buy the *...For Dummies* books you want online.
3. Get ten great *Dummies Tips*™ every week.
4. Chat with your favorite *...For Dummies* authors.
5. Subscribe free to *The Dummies Dispatch*™ newsletter.
6. Enter our sweepstakes and win cool stuff.
7. Send a free cartoon postcard to a friend.
8. Download free software.
9. Sample a book before you buy.
10. Talk to us. Make comments, ask questions, and get answers!

Jump online to these ten fun and useful things at
http://www.dummies.com/10useful

SURF THE NET

WWW.DUMMIES.COM

For other technology titles from IDG Books Worldwide, go to
www.idgbooks.com

Not online yet? It's easy to get started with *The Internet For Dummies*® 6th Edition, or *Dummies 101*®: *The Internet For Windows*® 98, available at local retailers everywhere.

IDG BOOKS WORLDWIDE

Find other *...For Dummies* books on these topics:
Business • Careers • Databases • Food & Beverages • Games • Gardening • Graphics
Hardware • Health & Fitness • Internet and the World Wide Web • Networking • Office Suites
Operating Systems • Personal Finance • Pets • Programming • Recreation • Sports
Spreadsheets • Teacher Resources • Test Prep • Word Processing

IDG BOOKS WORLDWIDE BOOK REGISTRATION

Register This Book and Win!

We want to hear from you!

Visit **http://my2cents.dummies.com** to register this book and tell us how you liked it!

- ✔ Get entered in our monthly prize giveaway.
- ✔ Give us feedback about this book — tell us what you like best, what you like least, or maybe what you'd like to ask the author and us to change!
- ✔ Let us know any other *...For Dummies*® topics that interest you.

Your feedback helps us determine what books to publish, tells us what coverage to add as we revise our books, and lets us know whether we're meeting your needs as a *...For Dummies* reader. You're our most valuable resource, and what you have to say is important to us!

Not on the Web yet? It's easy to get started with *Dummies 101*®*: The Internet For Windows*® *98* or *The Internet For Dummies*,® 6th Edition, at local retailers everywhere.

Or let us know what you think by sending us a letter at the following address:

...For Dummies Book Registration
Dummies Press
7260 Shadeland Station, Suite 100
Indianapolis, IN 46256-3917
Fax 317-596-5498

™

BESTSELLING
BOOK SERIES